100 Houses 100 Years

The Twentieth Century Society

Edited by Susannah Charlton
and Elain Harwood

BATSFORD

First published in the United Kingdom in 2017 by Batsford
43 Great Ormond Street
London WC1N 3HZ

An imprint of Pavilion Books Group

ISBN: 9781849944373

A CIP catalogue record for this book is available from the British Library.

10 9 8 7 6 5 4 3 2 1

Reproduction by Tag, UK
Printed by 1010 Printing International Ltd, China

This book can be ordered direct from the publisher at the website:
www.pavilionbooks.com or try your local bookshop.

All the houses are strictly private save where noted and most are not visible
from the street.

Page 2 The Black Rubber House by Simon Conder Associates in Dungeness, Kent (see page 180).

Contents

Above Sarah Peers and Jeremy Melling photographed at Brackenfell (see page 56) for the 'Me and My House' feature in the *C20 Magazine*.

Why do houses excite our emotions?

Catherine Croft

More than any type of building, our lives are influenced by houses – by the homes we live in and those we visit. When we organise C20 Society members' events, we can always be sure that a visit allowing access to the interior of private house will sell fast. I really enjoy writing the *C20 Magazine*'s 'Me and My House' features, (designed in part, if I am honest, as an excuse for me to visit some amazing places), and I particularly like hearing how people ended up living in a notable bit of twentieth-century design. Sometimes it is largely chance but it has frequently been the result of both extreme tenacity and enthusiasm, with quite often a dedication

to research and conservation bordering on the obsessive. Some embrace living a full-on period lifestyle, or at least develop a serious eBay habit, but most just love the extra light and space they have found, and frequently enjoy a more integrated relationship with outdoors, often in marked contrast to their previous Victorian or Georgian homes.

The houses I grew up in myself were comfortable but not very exciting. Family lore has it that my seemingly off-piste interest in architecture (not something anyone in my family had studied before) must have been prompted by Strawberry Hill House: I'm not so sure. Horace Walpole's Gothic home (now

Above The Span estate at Fieldend, Twickenham, London, completed 1960.

open to the public, but then gloomily mysterious and largely impenetrable) was immediately across the street from our 1920s suburban home. At that time it was a Roman Catholic teacher training college and when my mother had some part-time work there, she allegedly skimped on babysitters and left me in my pram to gaze at the ornate traceried ceilings. I have absolutely no recollection of this. I am not convinced that the then depressingly institutional character of the spaces had any impact on me. What I do remember is regularly going with my mother to her hairdressers in a light, sun-infused domestic space around the corner. This hairdresser worked from home, and her home (I know now) was part of a 1960 Span estate. Fieldend in Twickenham, London, was awarded a Housing Gold Award in 1961 and a Civic Trust Award in 1962. It felt like entering a different world. New Ash Green, a later Span development, takes our 1969 slot.

Today economic circumstances have led to an inevitable emphasis on the core investment value of houses, and political rhetoric has fuelled a gut feeling that financial security and social rootedness are linked to owning a house. At the same time, twentieth-century architects have become increasingly interested in the broader psychological impact of buildings on people, and particularly psychological readings of houses. An Englishman's home became not just his castle but an essential element of his self-perception and core inner being. Philosopher Gaston Bachelard writes in *The Poetics of Space* about how 'by remembering "houses" and "rooms", we learn to "abide" within ourselves'. Perhaps houses that were less compartmented might not only change how we physically spend our time but enable us to think in a more creative and free-flowing way. However, Bachelard saw verticality and concentrated centrality as key aspects of a house. I am struck by the fact that from the 1950s on, height and centrality were increasingly less consistent attributes of domestic architecture. The twentieth-century house becomes increasingly horizontal, more diffuse in form, and integrated into the landscape. The imagination of architects seems to leapfrog Bachelard. Maybe it is the sense of infinite possibility that draws us so strongly to want to know houses intimately.

Are C20 private houses 'at risk'?

Despite this popularity, the futures of even the best twentieth-century houses are not necessarily secure. My first major case at C20 was not a Brutalist car park or public housing estate but a classic 1930s modern movement house, threatened with complete demolition. Sadly, despite our best endeavours, Greenside, by Connell Ward and Lucas, 1937 was destroyed. I was surprised. I'd thought that 1930s buildings (especially ones which, like Greenside, were by well-known architects and were listed) were safe. I also thought that houses should be relatively simple to find conservation solutions for. After all the requirements for a house: sleeping, eating, living, have not essentially changed, and twentieth-century private houses have none of the problems of scale posed by vast eighteenth-century stately homes, such as Wentworth Woodhouse (recently offered £7.6m by the Chancellor). Not do they have the perceived negative social stigma associated with the large post-war housing estates. As this book shows, the house evolved a very long way during the twentieth century as lifestyles become less formal, servants became a rare luxury and women's roles changed. However we have seen many conservation issues prove common to houses from other decades, and Greenside demonstrated many of those we still come across most frequently.

Most notably, Greenside was a relatively modest and small house, surrounded by larger, more glamorous and more recent neighbours. It was chilly and poorly insulated, and hence expensive to run and environmentally profligate (although reducing a viable building to rubble is pretty bad news in terms of energy consumption too). It lacked a big kitchen, with room to sit and entertain, rather than just serve as a utilitarian workspace. With a bit of care and imagination (and, to be honest, a generous budget) all these problems could have been sensitively overcome, but sadly in the case of Greenside the bulldozers were brought in first. The experience taught me that frequently economics was going to argue against conservation. In sheer money terms it was far more profitable to knock down Greenside and build a new, larger house on the site, and the fine imposed on the owner for acting illegally in doing so was laughably small in relation to the profit to

Above Greenside, Virginia Water, Surrey, Connell Ward and Lucas, 1937, listed Grade II but demolished in 2003.

be made. The sums are even more compellingly in favour of redevelopment when two or more houses can be fitted on the plot (and often these houses had generous gardens so this is frequently possible).

Another major loss was the most radical of architect Edward Cullinan's early houses. This was designed for his uncle Mervyn Horder in rural Hampshire in 1958. It explored new technology in terms of integrating passive solar design, and combined self-build 'bricolage' and an almost deconstructivist formal language of tilted and twisted planes. An intensely urban house with a multi-layered history has been another recent loss, not demolished entirely but recently turned down for listing and extensively altered. This was Hornton Street, Kensington, unusual as a composite designed by James Melvin as his own home, reworked by Sauerbruch Hutton in 1994. It was featured in director Johanna Hogg's film *Exhibition* where it feels almost as vivid as the human characters.

The future of the twentieth-century house

All the more reason, then, to do all we can to make these houses better known and more desirable, and encourage more people to value them for what they are. To this end, three of the journals we've published are on houses: *The Modern House*, *Post-War Houses* and most recently simply *Houses*. The last looks at less extensively published architectural practices outside London where architects had managed to develop a cluster of individually commissioned houses at various dates. The chapter on Mervyn Seal's work around Torquay, including his dramatic 'butterfly roof' houses evolved directly out of casework – this time with a better outcome, which we were able to celebrate by running a couple of weekend visits to Devon to see them. *Post-War Houses* featured Robert Harvey's Frank Lloyd Wright-inspired work around Coventry, which has suffered as a result of the extreme wealth of the area: Stonecrop (built for himself between 1955 and 1957) narrowly escaped a massive extension

Above Still from the film *Exhibition* in which 60 Hornton Street, Kensington, London had a starring role.

when it was listed grade II★, but at South Winds (built in 1965) we were unable to prevent consent for an enormous extension on a scale that would never have been considered appropriate to an older listed house.

We also publish a series of books on individual architects, though so far, out of the eleven we have published, only Aldington, Craig and Collinge are known principally for their houses. Their 1971 Anderton House was acquired by the Landmark Trust in 2000, enabling holiday-makers to experience it first hand. Of course, houses certainly do appear in other books in the series, such as Powell and Moya's Martin's (1954), Leonard Manasseh's 6 Bacon's Lane (1959) and Trees by Ryder and Yates (1968), all featured here. Also among these 100 Houses are the work of forthcoming subjects in the series: Patrick Gwynne's The Homewood in 1939 (which belongs to the National Trust – one of a very few twentieth-century house museums in the UK) and Frederick Gibberd's BISF House in 1944.

We hope you will enjoy reading *100 Houses 100 Years* as much as we have enjoyed writing all the entries and debating what to include. Many wonderful houses have of course had to be left out and many architects we would have loved to represent are missing. This is just a taster, deliberately mixing the well-known with the deeply obscure, the avant-garde with the traditional, and safely protected buildings with ones still very much at risk. Our selection is designed to entice you to want to know more, to read further and, we hope, to join C20, to help us preserve twentieth-century architecture and come with us on future visits.

Catherine Croft
Director, C20 Society

Details of C20 events and publications and how to join the C20 Society can be found at www.c20society.org.uk

Above Architect Peter Aldington has established a trust to secure the future of his house and garden, Turn End in Haddenham, Buckinghamshire.

1914

Chestnut Grove

Architect: Raymond Unwin
Location: New Earswick, York
Status: Listed Grade II

New Earswick was developed as a Garden Village
for Rowntree employees by the Joseph Rowntree
Village Trust, formed in December 1905, with
Raymond Unwin (1863–1940) appointed as their
architect. The houses in Chestnut Grove were
built in 1910–14, compact three-bedroomed types,
with a living room and scullery on the ground
floor. Their design, however, dates back to c.1900,
when Raymond Unwin designed a pair of Voysey-
influenced cottages built in Church Stretton,
Shropshire. In 1902–03 these were combined into
a terrace of four, grouped with a Barry Parker-
designed pair in Western Terrace, the prototype
'pre-Trust' phase of New Earswick. These designs
were part of a series of type designs also used at
Letchworth and they set standards for the first half
of the twentieth century. Unfortunately updating
of services in the 1970s resulted in the loss of the
central chimneystacks from most housing in New
Earswick; a loss to the townscape.

Mervyn Miller

1915

129 Grosvenor Road

Architect: Sir Giles and Adrian Gilbert Scott
Location: Pimlico, London
Status: Demolished

Sir Giles Gilbert Scott made his name by winning the competition for Liverpool Anglican Cathedral at the age of 22, but he was much more than a Gothic church architect. Shortly before the First World War an opportunity arose for him to try out the modish 'Neo-Grec' style, that refined Greco-Roman manner, for a Thames-side house in Pimlico. The client was the Hon. Sir Arthur Stanley, MP, who took his young architect to Italy first, and Pompeii was clearly the theme in what was built in 1913–15 (with the assistance of Scott's younger architect brother, Adrian). Stanley was disabled, so all the house was on one floor, with rooms arranged around an open atrium with a Greek Doric *stoa* overlooking the river. Scott also designed furniture which reveals him as a pioneer in the Regency Revival. This house was not an unqualified success: Thames bargees stole the cushions, the atrium was soon roofed over and, much altered, it finally disappeared at the end of the twentieth century.

Gavin Stamp

1916

Royd House

Architect: Edgar Wood
Location: 224 Hale Road, Hale, Cheshire
Status: Listed Grade I

Edgar Wood's own house is theatrical and exotic: it amused him, on arrival at the local station, to tell the cabbie to take him to 'the ugliest house in Hale'.

From the street a dished gateway in a high brick wall leads to an imposing circular courtyard. The house front is symmetrical with curved external walls and a tiled panel influenced by his 1914 tour of Tunisia and Persia. The roof is flat, the plan part way between Art Nouveau butterfly and modern. Inside the house, silk Mandarin gowns were used as wall hangings, and the kitchen was in turquoise and gold leaf. Sadly these are lost, but a fractal Arabic-style door and ceiling painted by Wood himself can still be seen in the circular hall.

With its unity of plan and landscape, Royd House prefigured the Riviera house Wood built for himself in 1932 at Porto Maurizio where he spent his last years painting.

Andrew Crompton

1917

All Hallows

Architect: F.C. Eden
Location: The Green, Ardeley, Hertfordshire
Status: Listed Grade II

The Green, a horseshoe of houses and a parish hall built around a functional well, is the principal feature of the small village of Ardeley. It is based on Blaise Hamlet, Bristol: a picturesque scheme by John Nash of 1811. All Hallows, one of two detached houses and the first to be completed, owes little to the Regency *cottage orné* being rooted in the Arts and Crafts tradition. Sentimental decorative detail is avoided, as is any affectation of rusticity, giving an English picturesque dependent on materials, design and a sense of place rather than on whimsy or artifice.

All Hallows was inhabited by nuns until 1942, part of an Anglo-Catholic vision for Ardeley. The creation of workers' housing in an idyllic English setting at the height of the First World War gave the scheme an added pathos articulated by a painted inscription on one of the houses: *auspicium meloris aevi*: 'a sign of better times.'

Edward Hagger

1918

77 High Street

Architect: Orphoot and Whiting
Location: Clovelly, Devon
Status: Listed Grade II

Zachary Hamlyn, born locally, made his fortune as a lawyer and purchased the Clovelly estate in 1738. It passed by descent to Christine Hamlyn Fane, who in 1889 married Frederick Gosling, whom she persuaded to adopt the name Hamlyn. She also convinced him to devote his considerable fortune to restoring the village, then in poor repair and without sanitation. Many houses were altered between 1914 and 1925 and, while the village appears ancient, datestones with the initials 'C.H.' reveal the truth. No.77 is basically eighteenth-century, but with twentieth-century windows, a concrete balcony and a flat roof at the rear. If architects were involved it was perhaps the firm of Orphoot and Whiting of Bideford and London; a later partner was Ian Lindsay, responsible for more sophisticated restoration work in Scottish villages. Hamlyn's friends included Rex Whistler, who produced designs for Wedgwood and for textiles based on the village.

Elain Harwood

1919

156–8 Cressing Road

Architect: C.H.B. Quennell and W.F. Crittall
Location: Braintree, Essex
Status: Listed Grade II

Easily overlooked with their nearly ubiquitous modern disguise of PVC windows and pastel render, sitting in a sea of hard standing and parked cars, this group of mostly semi-detached cottages holds enormous importance as pioneer British modernist housing. The houses were built by the Crittall Manufacturing Company immediately after the First World War for the workforce at Crittall's Manor Works nearby in Coggeshall Road, Braintree. Designed by C.H. Quennell and W.F. Crittall, the cottages were built between 1918 and 1920. Flat-roofed (in reinforced concrete) and constructed on a metric concrete block system they also proudly demonstrated the qualities of Crittall's novel steel casement windows, of which they were pioneer manufacturers. The group has particular resonance when seen as the precursor to the far more ambitious, resolved and well-planned modernist housing within the factory village at Silver End (see page 38), acting as a highly effective, eye-catching advertisement for the product.

Gillian Darley

1920

Laughton Lodge

Architect: C.F.A. Voysey
Location: Laughton, near Market Harborough, Leicestershire
Status: Listed Grade II

Laughton Hills is a testament to the singular vision and intransigence of C.F.A. Voysey. The celebrated architect was 63 in 1920 when the house and laboratory were commissioned by William Taylor for a site at Laughton. Initially only the Lodge, a laboratory, was constructed. It was Taylor who put the dimples into golf balls. He was an engineer and golf ball manufacturer, and his innovation, based on the observation that old and pitted golf balls outperformed smooth new ones, was revolutionary.

Taylor adapted Voysey's design when he built the house in 1935. Voysey's extraordinary building accentuates the Gothic origins of his design philosophy in defiance of changing architectural fashions. His characteristic roughcast render elevations with stone mullioned windows, grouped in horizontal bands, have castellated parapets and the house is distinguished by a playful tower. It was designed from his home, a small flat in St James's Street, London, after his office was relinquished during the First World War.

Wendy Hitchmough

1921

The Tudor Cottage

Architect: Ernest Trobridge
Location: Harrow, Middlesex
Status: Listed Grade II

Trobridge was an architect who used traditional building materials out of necessity rather than whimsy. Due to a lack of affordable building materials following the First World War, he developed a prototype using green elm for wooden houses that were fast and cheap to build, required no scaffolding or foundations, and could be constructed on-site by unskilled labour. Framework was standardised and fenestration could be inserted wherever required, allowing for great flexibility in design: adaptable to both the client's requirements and the creativity of the architect.

A committed Swedenborgian, Trobridge's religious philosophy permeates his work. The hearth as a symbol for family and home can be read from outside – many of his houses have extravagant chimneys. This house in Harrow has a particularly good one. Together with a double pitched roof, irregular windows and bays at each floor, and cladding of red tile and ribbons of roughly cut elm, it certainly lives up to its name.

Tess Pinto

1922

Cour

Architect: Oliver Hill
Location: Carradale, Argyll and Bute
Status: Listed Grade A

An astonishing country house' says the listing entry for Cour, and it is – for its remote location overlooking the Isle of Bute, for its massive stonework, its generosity of internal scale and its primitivism of style. It is Scottish in some details, but seen through a tough abstract version of the Arts and Crafts movement, with premonitions of Hill's future of love of curved walls and wide low doorways. The client was a mysterious Mr J.B. Gray, in the shipping business.

Oliver Hill's career blossomed briefly before he joined the London Scottish Regiment and endured four years in the trenches. Cour was the house with which he began his path to stardom as a fashionable interwar stylist with a heart in the Highlands. He came and camped alone on the site for two weeks before beginning the design. Local whinstone was quarried for the walls, but it has proved almost impossible to keep dry.

Alan Powers

1923

Coedfa

Architect: Herbert Luck North
Location: The Close, Llanfairfechan, Gwynedd
Status: Listed Grade II

Steep, paired gables almost became a North trademark, along with his roughcast walls, cottage windows and thick slate roofs. Never ostentatious, always practical and with an eye to the past, North, who worked for a while with Lutyens, found his style early and rarely strayed from it. Gothic was the only architectural period that North would countenance, and at Coedfa we see his typical arched doorways and fireplace surrounds.

Coedfa forms part of a 'village' of small, modest houses that North developed from 1898 right up until his death in 1941. He lived nearby, at Wern Isaf (1900) and worked, usually alone, from a bedroom there. In many ways, the village was his built vision of the celestial city, picturesque houses built on the hillside around a field, along with a church institute, a working men's club and a small college for girls, with its imposing chapel (demolished, alas, in 1970).

Adam Voelcker

Church Rate Corner

Architect: Hugh Mackay Baillie Scott
Location: Cambridge
Status: Listed Grade II

This house was designed in 1924 for Mrs A.H.N. Sewell by Baillie Scott and Beresford, that is, by the Arts and Crafts architect Hugh Mackay Baillie Scott who, like C.F.A. Voysey, had made his name at the turn of the century with his sensible houses and his decorative work. After the Edwardian years he, like Voysey, began to be seen by some as reactionary because of his dislike of the new modernism. 'Instead of turning his back on the splendid work of his fathers', he wrote, let the modern architect 'find inspiration in the buildings which have given us the precious heritage of rural England.' But Baillie Scott carried on building extensively after the First World War. He designed several houses in Cambridge, of which this is the most abstract, with a timeless traditional character achieved through plain, lime-washed walls, the arrangement of roof planes, gables and oak-framed leaded-light windows. Cleverly and compactly planned, and superbly built, it shows how simple, unaffected modernity could be achieved by well-tried means – and fine craftsmanship.

Gavin Stamp

What makes these houses special?

Elain Harwood

What is it that makes us watch *Grand Designs* or scroll through the Modern House and WowHaus websites, even though most of us can only dream of building or buying a state-of-the-art house? Once there was only the distant country house to idolise, but the twentieth century introduced a second kind of beautiful house, smaller but a work of art, to which the contents were subordinate or – better still – built-in to form a cohesive whole. They are the collective product of a creative elite of architects, artists and their clients, and they reflect the changing culture of the twentieth century. Most are beautiful rather than luxurious, and some of the most interesting were built as low-cost public housing or for wartime munitions workers.

The beguilement of the small house is as old as the linotype printing and half-tone block that made possible magazines like the *Architectural Review* and *Country Life*, founded in 1896 and 1897 respectively, which promoted the new middle-class homes. *Country Life* recognised their seduction when it championed the work of Edwin Lutyens and thence that of the Arts and Crafts Movement, which stands as a prequel to the houses erected from

1914 onwards. A.H. Mackmurdo and Edgar Wood introduced the flat roof and moved towards more simply moulded façades, while Lutyens and younger architects advanced refinement towards classical orthodoxy. The 1920s saw both neo-classical and modern strands advance in the face of a rock-bottom economy when house building was limited.

The *Daily Mail* launched the Ideal Home Exhibition in 1908, in recognition that more people could afford to own their own homes and still more were looking to buy attractive furnishings, and in 1922 built an enclave of decent semi-detached houses at Welwyn Garden City, Hertfordshire. *Ideal Home* first appeared in 1920, suggesting that magazines flourish when there is no money to build. The American *House and Garden* launched a separate British edition in 1946 to 'provide new stimulus, guidance and example' to homeowners re-planning their lifestyles after the Second World War.

American models became important in Britain, as books and magazines sped ideas back and forth across the Atlantic. The Arts and Crafts Movement had reinvented the medieval great hall as a multi-purpose living room, but it was Americans like Henry Hobson Richardson, Bernard Maybeck and Frank Lloyd Wright who opened out the house into fluid interlocking spaces defined only by a fireplace, cabinet or stair. In Britain, Charles Voysey was among the first to develop the hall on similar lines independently. French windows and sweeping loggias extended this fluidity into the garden, and as buildings became lighter and windows larger so architects explored the conceit of indoor/outdoor spaces where sliding glass and continuous floorings dissolved one into the other. Central heating advanced only slowly in Britain – Voysey hated it – but in Europe cellular plans, each room with a specific function, gave way to single large spaces with many uses. It is this breaking down of boxes into looser spaces where the imagination can take flight

Above Brooklyn, Private Road, Enfield, London, 1887 by A.H. Mackmurdo, a prototype modern house with a flat roof.

Above Houses in Meadow Green, Welwyn Garden City, built in 1922 for the *Daily Mail* in association with the Ideal Home Exhibition.

that sets modernism, and thereby the twentieth-century house, apart. British tastes remained eclectic through the 1930s, but the Modern Movement houses built in increasing numbers best served more active, informal lifestyles, with larger windows giving more light and fresh air, open areas for sunbathing, fitted bathrooms and dressing rooms. Patrick Gwynne modelled his single, large living room at The Homewood on that by Mies van der Rohe for the Tugendhats in Brno, with a sprung floor for dancing. The Homewood does have a separate dining room, shielded by a sliding partition, but elsewhere kitchen-diners and lounge living were preferred as the drinks party prevailed over the formal dinner until the late 1970s.

Although dependence on servants was declining, most middle-class households retained at least a 'daily' through the 1930s. A million servants quietly disappeared with the Second World War for greater independence in the armed forces and munitions factories, never to return. The housewife had to cook and clean for herself thereafter, but in return there was no need for the family to conceal itself within the home, so the last barriers to open-planning

broke down. The need for space for more hobbies in the home, and for children to do their homework, was recognised by the Parker Morris report *Homes for Today and Tomorrow* published in 1961, whose recommended space standards became a statutory minimum for public housing by 1969. It laid great emphasis on central heating as a means of using the home more efficiently. Energy fell in price and was expected to become still cheaper, so that the lifestyle of the French Riviera and American movies could be enacted in all but the chilliest British climates. The third great change of the post-war era was the ready availability for the first time of large sheets of glass, thanks to Pilkington's advances in float glass technology.

The first post-war private houses were necessarily modest as building restrictions limited their cost and size, so that building materials in short supply could be directed towards schools, industry and public housing. In 1945 the maximum size allowed was 1,000sq ft (92.9sq m), with 930sq ft (86.4sq m) for a bungalow; they could cost no more than £1,400 in London and £1,300 elsewhere. Following a run

Above John Winter's own house, 81 Swain's Lane, Highgate, London, 1968–69.

on the pound, Stafford Cripps imposed further cuts in 1947, and forbade private building save for key workers. Conditions eased in subsequent years and houses up to 1,500sq ft (139.4sq m) were permitted, but restrictions remained in force until November 1954. Then Harold Macmillan, Minister of Housing and Local Government, 'set the builders free'. Most volume housing was repetitious, wasteful of space and expensive to heat, and by March 1961, when Ian Nairn made a ferocious attack in the *Architectural Review*, was spreading rapidly to create yet more of what he had earlier termed 'Subtopia'. 'The speculative builder is on the march again, whenever the planning authority will let him, despoiling the countryside as ruthlessly and thoughtlessly as he did before the war'. Never let it be forgotten that the houses in this book are the exceptional ones. Architects, whether working for local authorities or on one-off houses, could produce compact yet imaginative designs with windows that were just a little bigger, eaves that were a little lower, and a more careful relationship with the landscape. The

retention of existing trees and topography was a major concern, even on sites where old buildings were ruthlessly demolished.

National Service enabled many architects to explore Western Europe during leave periods, while others ventured to Denmark or Sweden and the most intrepid to the USA. Here was the greatest inspiration for new private houses and consumer goods, encouraged by the lifestyles seen in films or on television, in magazines and the highly coloured ads collected by the proponents of Pop Art and Brutalism. Marcel Breuer, Walter Gropius and their circles offered a contemporary style in a wide palette of materials, while Frank Lloyd Wright's Usonian houses showed how brick and timber could be used simply and naturally, yet beautifully. Mies van der Rohe's Farnsworth House near Chicago was an introduction to steel, its tiny scale adding to its allure. But the greatest sources of inspiration were the Case Study Houses of southern California, a programme initiated by John Entenza, editor of *Arts and Architecture* to fill his pages and attract advertising from suppliers.

A series of lightweight single-storey houses, mostly steel-framed but including a few of timber, were briefly open to the public and published in detail. The seductive photographs by Julius Shulman depicted flowing living rooms, many with sunken conversation areas to give greater height, leading to well-planned kitchens and sun-drenched terraces with glimpses of a pool or limousine beyond. The first houses, in the late 1940s, were intended for modest incomes, but many later ones were frankly luxurious – literally the Hollywood lifestyle of the movies.

England responded with the *House and Garden* 'House of Ideas' and *Woman's Journal* 'House of the Year', beginning in 1956 and 1957 respectively. The first *Woman's Journal* houses were mock-ups in department stores to demonstrate interior designs by Michael Inchbald, but from 1959 the magazine chose a real house from an estate of executive homes or commissioned its own house for an imaginary family. Most women's magazines included articles on decorating the home, and advanced by 1960 to feature modern design, as when the modest *Home* magazine commissioned a column from José Manser, whose architect husband Michael specialised in open-plan steel-framed houses in the latest American style. Janet Street-Porter began her media career as home editor for *Petticoat* magazine, producing features on student housing by Farrell and Grimshaw as well as DIY projects for the teenage bedroom.

Patrick Gwynne and Michael Manser were among many architects who built houses for themselves or close relatives. Here they enjoyed the freedom to act as their own clients, to build for the lifestyle they wanted to lead, and the results were splendid advertisements for their skills. Architects'

Above Domus, Colne Road, Reedley, Burnley, by Alan Chambers for Eric Cookson, a local builder. The basement bar is original.

homes were among the most published of modern houses in post-war Britain and, still more than the Case Study Houses, showed what could be done by near-penniless couples on tiny budgets.

Open planning was easier where there was no need to support an upper floor. Living areas could be bigger, skylights could focus light where it was most needed and allow rooms to be deeper; bedrooms were not constrained by the floor below, and more could be added as required. A distinctive feature of both single- and multi-storey houses was the separation of spaces for parents and children. Children got a wing or basement close to the garden, with handy access for a pram and perhaps a room for an au pair. An early example is the house built in Avenue Road, Leicester, for Harold and Joan Goddard and their three children, where in 1955 the children had their own wing, and later a separate pavilion for hobbies or homework. In multi-storey houses, quiet adult spaces were generally at the top, sometimes including a study and a second,

smarter, lounge. Neave Brown's terrace of five houses at Winscombe Street, built in 1965–66 is an excellent example of what could be done on a tiny site, each unit only 14ft3in (4.3m) wide. Other houses incorporated workshops or more gregarious recreational spaces, as in Burnley, Lancashire, where the local developer Eric Cookson built himself a house of white concrete and brick that featured its own bar and glass dance floor. As all but the very elderly or those with very large families enjoyed more disposable income – for political pressures kept council rents low through the 1960s – so more could be spent on luxuries, seen when the cost of living index for 1962 featured for the first time sherry and frozen chicken as well as fish fingers.

The 1970s saw a sea-change in house building, thanks to a declining economy and a quadrupling of oil prices. John Winter recalled a decline in the building of architects' own homes, reversed only in the 1990s. The new private house assumed the vanguard of energy conservation, with thick walls

Above 22 Avenue Road, Leicester by Fello Atkinson and Brenda Walker 1953–55.

Above Cedarwood, Woolton, Liverpool, the *Woman's Journal* House of the Year for 1960.

and a judicious use of south-facing conservatories to retain heat without excessive solar gain; attempts to harness the sun and wind more actively to generate power have been less effective. A return to more massive structures and a reaction to modernism's excesses encouraged post-modernism, with playful brickwork and a greater use of colour, and briefly a return to a greater formalism of plan. However, in the 1990s the private house launched a modernist revival, tempered by energy efficiency and softer materials such as weatherboarding and render alongside steel. The most adventurous recent houses are for singletons or empty-nesters, dominated by a large living kitchen or a workspace where children's needs have become secondary. Whether in volume

house building or in one-off houses, the skill today is to squeeze onto ever tinier sites a house that offers privacy yet sociability, with the dining table as its centrepiece. Such a house respects its neighbours without compromising a modern aesthetic that emphasises an abstract shape. The House for Essex (see page 200) is shocking because its personification of the fictional Julie Cope stands so against the grain of anonymous black outlines and clean voids found elsewhere this century, houses that expect us to exert our own imaginations as to how we might live there – precisely why they are so enticing.

1925

Gledstone Hall

Architect: Sir Edwin Lutyens
Location: Skipton, Yorkshire
Status: Listed Grade II*

Gledstone Hall is one of the few houses designed
by Sir Edwin Lutyens, doyen of English domestic
architects, after the First World War when he was
busy with war memorials and urban buildings. The
client was Sir Amos Nelson, a cotton mill owner,
who first asked the local architect Richard Jacques
to reconstruct an existing Yorkshire country house.
Jacques, asked to collaborate with someone of greater
experience, then suggested Lutyens. At Gledstone,
built in 1923–26 on a different site, Surrey and
the English vernacular are forgotten. The house is
classical and rigidly symmetrical, even (unusually)
in plan. There is something of the formality of
New Delhi about it, while Lutyens's biographer,
Christopher Hussey, thought he put 'something of
the France of Louis XVI into Yorkshire'. But, with
its tall first-floor windows and high pitched roof, the
house has a distinctive character and, inside, Lutyens
played games with black and white marble. Lutyens's
long formal garden was the last to be planted with
the advice of Gertrude Jekyll.

Gavin Stamp

1926

New Ways

Architect: Peter Behrens
Location: 508 Wellingborough Road, Northampton
Status: Listed Grade II*

New Ways established a link between modern domestic architecture, health and efficiency in Britain. Built for businessman W.J.Bassett-Lowke, stalwart of the Design and Industries Association, it incorporated his ideas about modern living with highly individual features designed by Peter Behrens by correspondence. By this time, Behrens had moved away from classicism and embraced Expressionist ideas. Using furniture previously designed by C.R. Mackintosh for Bassett-Lowke, and purchases from the 1925 Paris Exhibition, architect and client created a series of striking, colourful interiors. These, its flat roof and south-facing rear balconies, led critics to view New Ways as a pioneer of modern architecture in Britain. Yet in spite of its stylish décor, advanced domestic equipment and jazzy fenestration, the cement-rendered house had conventional cavity brick walls. Silver Street (see page 38) reveals the importance of New Ways, not as a forerunner of the International Style but as offering a robust alternative to designers and providers of housing.

Louise Campbell

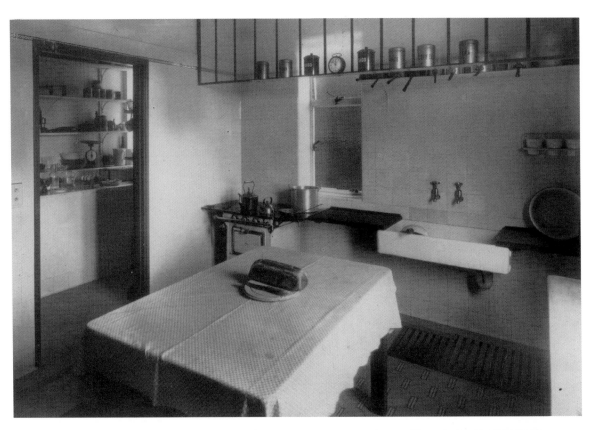

1927

Silver Street

Architect: Tait and MacManus of Sir John Burnet and Partners
Location: Silver End, Essex
Status: Listed Grade II

Inspired by New Ways, (see page 34) Silver Street was the first group of houses in the UK in the European modernist style. White, cubic and flat-roofed, three detached houses, a group of 24 semi-detached and two terraces of four were designed by Thomas Tait (1882–1954) and Frederick MacManus (1903–85) as part of a larger estate for the workforce of Crittall Windows.

Although modernist in appearance the houses were traditional in plan and construction, with brick walls painted white, but with concrete lintels allowing a wider fenestration displaying to their best the sleek metal window frames.

Crittall windows had been used by Burnet and Partners in London buildings such as Vigo House (c.1920) and Adelaide House (1925), and became a feature of many modernist buildings worldwide: the Bauhaus, Dessau (1926), the Hoover Building in London (1933), Falling Water, Pennsylvania (1935), and Finsbury Health Centre, London (1938).

Dennis Wardleworth

Tudor Close

Architect: C.W. Neville and A.Caplin
Location: Rottingdean, East Sussex
Status: Listed Grade II

There is a case to be made that Neo-Tudor is the only national English style and the principal representative domestic manner of the twentieth century. Notably popular between the World Wars for suburban houses in particular, this half-timbered architecture was often given extra romance and appealing texture by using recycled materials. Tudor Close is a fine example: a three-sided court of seven houses built in 1924–28 by C.W. Neville of the South Coast Land and Resort Co. It was designed by A. Caplin, an amateur enthusiast and restorer, who used old oak timbers from broken-up ships and old barns, recycled bricks and flint and 'mossy tiles' combined with new oak carvings. For P.A. Barron, author of *The House Desirable* (1929), 'you will find it very hard to believe that the buildings were not erected in the distant days of Henry VIII, or Queen Elizabeth.' Such engaging Olde Worlde fakery appealed to Hollywood as, soon converted for a time into an hotel, Tudor Close became a favourite with the likes of Bette Davis and Cary Grant.

Gavin Stamp

1929

Finella

Architect: Raymond McGrath
Location: Queen's Road, Cambridge
Status: Listed Grade II*

If the Modern Movement in Britain had a birthplace, it was in the twin drawing rooms at Finella, a Victorian house converted for an eccentric don by a shy genius from Australia. Poets, politicians, social entrepreneurs, educationalists, rugby players and social butterflies were drawn by Mansfield Forbes's hospitality and his desire to make the world a finer, more tolerant place. Wired and silvered glass, Induroleum and copper Plymax glittered with occult suggestiveness, invoking Finella, the Scottish queen who invented glass but died in a waterfall. Cambridge academia was astonished, especially when Forbes displayed Epstein's sculpture Genesis during May Week to raise money for saving a historic windmill.

The 'Three Musketeers' – McGrath, Wells Coates and Serge Chermayeff – met here and went on to greater things. Forbes died in 1935 and the décor suffered, before partial restoration in the early 1980s.

Alan Powers

1930

High and Over

Architect: Amyas Connell in partnership with Stewart Lloyd Thomson
Location: Amersham, Buckinghamshire
Status: Listed Grade II*

The modernity of this gleaming white flat-roofed house, once prominent on a bare hilltop, attracted huge media attention. In 1928 the archaeologist Sir Bernard Ashmole, departing as director of the British School in Rome, poached architectural scholar Amyas Connell from the school by commissioning him to design a family house. The exploratory design of High and Over intermeshes their preoccupations, referencing the buildings of ancient Rome and the Renaissance and Connell's Beaux Arts and Arts and Crafts training. It symbolised a commitment to a modern solution.

High and Over's distinctive Y-shaped plan was devised to maximise daylight with three narrow wings radiating from the hexagonal central hall. The house has a reinforced concrete frame with infill brick and render over, like a unifying icing. This prefigured Connell's later purely poured reinforced concrete buildings in practice with Basil Ward and Colin Lucas. The original Italianate landscape scheme incorporated a lodge building and a water tower (now demolished).

Sally Rendel

1931

Sir Arthur Dorman Memorial Homes, 1–20 Dorman's Crescent

Architect: Mr J. Locking, Borough Engineer
Location: Dormanstown, Redcar
Status: Listed Grade II

Redcar prided itself as a seaside resort but much of its early twentieth-century prosperity came from the Dorman, Long and Company steelworks. The company had begun Dormanstown in 1917–20 to plans mainly by Stanley Adshead, and in 1929 it sold land there cheaply for council housing. So the borough was prepared when, in 1930, Ramsay MacDonald's Labour Government repealed the ancient Poor Laws and introduced a Housing Act permitting local authorities to build cottages for 'aged persons'. The borough engineer, Mr J. Locking, prepared plans and George Lansbury, Minister of Health, attended the laying of the foundation stone by Sir Alfred Dorman on 3 January 1931. When completed that May, the three terraces of one-bedroom cottages round a small green, each costing £209 5s to build, were the first by any council specifically for elderly couples. Renovated and with central heating, there is still a strong community of pensioners there.

Elain Harwood

1932

High Cross House

Architect: William Lescaze
Location: Dartington, Totnes, Devon
Status: Listed Grade II*

High Cross House (the headmaster's house) on the Dartington Estate is one of the first and best examples of the International Style in the UK. It is a smooth rendered, flat-roofed, geometric construction designed by the Swiss-born architect William Lescaze, who also specified the colours and finishes, internal furniture and fittings to create a complete essay in modernism. Lescaze was recommended to the owners, Dorothy and Leonard Elmhirst, by the new headmaster of Dartington Hall School, William Curry. Lescaze was most famous for designing the Philadelphia Saving Fund Building (1932), regarded as the first modernist skyscraper in the USA.

The school was part of the Elmhirst's venture in rural regeneration and education based at the ancient Dartington Hall Estate. Sadly this venture was not to last beyond their tenure and the school closed in 1987. Despite restoration in 1994 by John Winter, High Cross is now empty and in need of renovation once more.

Tony Stokoe

1933

2 Bata Avenue

Architect: Bata building department, headed by
Vladimir Karfik or Karfik and Gahura
Location: East Tilbury, Essex
Status: Listed Grade II

Tucked away in the Essex flatlands beyond the River Thames is an unexpected example of Czech Modernism. Thomas Bata, co-founder of the global shoe empire that continues today, had the vision of a British satellite built on the same lines as the main company town, Zlin. This became one of a number of industrial colonies built across several continents, characterised by functionalist architecture and garden city planning. In East Tilbury, the factory came first, followed by a cul-de-sac of flat-roofed, white-walled houses, partly concrete and partly rendered brick, all designed in Zlin. Even the window frames and electrical fittings were imported. No.2 Bata Avenue was built as one of a pair of hostels for single workers, reflecting the company preference for taking on and training up young recruits.

Despite change and loss, 'Bataville' remains proud of its international character, maintaining a cultural connection with the Bata organisation and continuing to attract attention for its architecture.

Joanna Smith

1934

64 Heath Drive

Architect: Francis Skinner and Tecton
Location: Gidea Park, Essex
Staus: Listed Grade II

Designed by Francis ('Freddie') Skinner when he was only 25, the house at Heath Drive was part of the Gidea Park Modern Homes Exhibition promoting architect-designed houses to compete with the conventional spec-built product. Skinner's prize-winning entry is clearly influenced by the pioneering examples he had seen on his continental travels. The reinforced concrete envelope, expressed columns, flat roof and screened terrace rehearse key elements of the Corbusian vocabulary. Most inventive is the L-shaped plan, which was intended to enable a row-house development with a continuous street frontage and a series of semi-enclosed gardens – a model unrealised here due to site constraints. The house nonetheless stands as an innovative and intriguing document of the early Modern Movement that, alongside Lubetkin's contemporaneous project at Genesta Road, Greenwich, represents an almost unique attempt to explore the terraced house form in a modern idiom as against the more prevalent single villa typology.

John Allan

1935

Torilla

Architect: F.R.S. Yorke
Location: Wilkins Green Lane, Hatfield, Hertfordshire
Status: Listed Grade II*

This beautiful white house was F.R.S. Yorke's very first house design and has an outstanding interior space. It was built by my grandmother Christabel for one of her children returning from Australia to the UK.

It has withstood numerous threats; during the Second World War it was said that Nazi bombers used it as a marker when bombing the neighbouring De Havilland factory; bought after the war, it was only saved from demolition to provide a site for two houses following letters from David Allford and myself; then it was saved from decomposition by John Winter, who renewed the very thin concrete and waterproofed and insulated the walls and the roof.

Finally a painter and his wife moved in and continued its restoration by adding a beautifully curved studio and finding much of the original furniture. In this short story you see how people were both far-sighted and optimistic in dark times.

Richard Burton

1936

East Wall

Architect: Elisabeth Benjamin with Godfrey Samuel
Location: 8 Hedgerley Lane, Gerrards Cross, Buckinghamshire
Status: Listed Grade II

East Wall represents the surge of modernist influence in British schools of architecture in the early 1930s and its galvanising effect on the first generation of women architectural students and professionals. Elisabeth Benjamin absorbed modernist principles and ideas from fellow Architectural Association students who went on to found the group Tecton, including Godfrey Samuel, a collaborator on East Wall. A member of the Modern Architectural Association (MARS) Group, Benjamin looked to the experimental, innovative approach of Le Corbusier, Gropius and the Bauhaus, while breaking the cubic box at East Wall with curvilinear forms and introducing concentrations of colour and texture with unpainted sewer brick.

Called the St George and Dragon House by its architects, an International Style building conceived metaphorically may seem a contradiction. Nonetheless, its reinforced concrete structure (St George astride) was one of the earliest domestic examples and the sinuous line of the brickwork (the Dragon) generated an evocative spiral staircase tower and an apsidal-ended dining room with generous terrace above.

Lynne Walker

1937

The Wood House

Architect: Walter Gropius
Location: Shipbourne, Kent
Status: Listed Grade II

Walter Gropius, leading European modern architect and founder of the Bauhaus, lived and worked in England from 1934–37. Although he was not Jewish the Nazi regime was hostile to the aesthetic values Gropius espoused and he hoped for better possibilities for work in England. As it turned out this was a forlorn hope.

The Wood House is one of just three buildings commissioned from Gropius while he was in England, the others being Impington Village College and 66 Old Church Street in Chelsea. The Wood House has the distinction of being Gropius's only English country house.

Gropius's clients were a left-wing intellectual couple, Jack and Frances Donaldson. The house was built on a 3 acre (1.2ha) site giving long, sloping views over fields and woodland. The building has a beautiful precision with its red cedar cladding, semi-formal entrance porch and outdoor sleeping terrace reached by external stairway. Here we see the beginnings of an architectural idiom Gropius perfected in his own house at Lincoln in New England once he moved from England to the USA.

Fiona MacCarthy

1938

Brackenfell

Architect: Leslie Martin and Sadie Speight
Location: Brampton, Cumbria
Status: Listed Grade II

This is a house with both fascinating designers and a very design-minded client. Alistair Morton, director of Edinburgh Weavers, commissioned artists including Ben and Winifred Nicholson to design fabrics for his family firm, and Leslie Martin and Sadie Speight as architects for a rural family home, compete with a spacious studio for himself.

Its hilltop setting in North Cumbria makes the most of views south to Helvellyn and the Lake District. It is approached from the north, where a circular driveway leads to the entrance, screened by a curved wall of local stone. It is more contextual than many interwar modernist houses. Ten years later Martin was to design the Royal Festival Hall, and in 1953 he became chief architect of the London County Council. But in the late 1930s he was head of architecture at Hull University and running a private practice with his wife and former fellow student. Speight's career deserves further study: as well as co-writing *The Flat Book* (1939), she and Martin built or extended a number of houses.

Catherine Croft

1939

The Homewood

Architect: Patrick Gwynne
Location: Esher, Surrey
Status: Listed Grade II

Patrick Gwynne was only 24 when he designed The Homewood to replace the Victorian property his family already occupied on the site. The luxurious principal rooms are set on the first floor to enjoy views over the luscious 10 (4ha) acre garden, itself largely the work of Gwynne and his father. The bedrooms are arranged in a separate wing raised on pilotis to form a *porte-cochère*, and joined to the main block by a glazed link enclosing a ceremonial spiral staircase. The numerous built-in fittings and most of the furniture were also designed by the architect. After the Second World War Gwynne returned to The Homewood where he based his practice and remained, subtly adapting and refining it, for the rest of his 90-year life. Now owned by the National Trust, The Homewood presents the most complete record of its period of a modern architect's personal domestic vision to be found anywhere in England.

John Allan

1940

Harbour Meadow

Architect: Peter Moro and Richard Llewelyn Davies with Gordon Cullen
Location: Birdham, Chichester
Status: Listed Grade II

This generous property on a fine, secluded site by Birdham Creek is one of the most sophisticated and luxurious modern houses of the interwar period. Peter Moro and Gordon Cullen had both worked in Tecton and the influence of Berthold Lubetkin is pervasive. The plan is configured in two parallel wings segregating the main reception rooms, study and master bedroom nearer the waterside, from the kitchen, service areas, family and guest bedrooms overlooking the driveway. The central link contains a virtuoso spiral staircase. Entered through a proscenium opening in the covered walkway connecting the house with the garage, a planted courtyard forms an outdoor ante-room to the main entrance. The interior was fully fitted out by the architects with many inventive details, including a faux neo-classical window by Cullen framing the waterside view from the dining room. A restoration of the property was completed by Avanti Architects in 2005.

John Allan

2 Mayor's Close, Canley

Architect: Donald Gibson
Location: Coventry, West Midlands

The suburb of Canley began to be developed with traditional semis in 1939, when, as everywhere, building stopped as materials were commandeered for the war effort. Yet Coventry desperately needed housing as workers flocked to its munitions factories. The city architect, Donald Gibson, snuck through 42 flat-roofed brick houses in and off Sheriff Avenue, completed in December 1941 with concrete roof joists and stairs because timber was so scarce. Most were built in fours, set forward and back for variety and with a central entry serving the middle houses, reserving semis for the ends. Alterations have savaged their austere good looks save for the end house, whose concrete porch and yellow tiles show how a dash of joviality was important in such hard times.

Canley offers a smorgasbord of ration-book housing. Gibson's prototype two-storey 'Coventry prefab' has gone, but there remains a tin town of BISF housing like that in Northolt, Middlesex (see page 66).

Elain Harwood

1942

Heol Pant y Rhyn and Lon-y-Celyn

Architect: Geoffrey Jellicoe
Location: Whitchurch, Cardiff

The 'phoney' war of 1939–40 gave the Government time to build new ordnance factories in the west of England and Wales. Thousands of workers were recruited, but then found they had nowhere to live. The Ministry of Supply built huts and hostels for single people, and commissioned 3,448 terraced and semi-detached houses for families from known housing specialists. Jellicoe established a reputation in this field with seven estates of flat-roofed brick houses, mainly terraced and distinctive for their boldly projecting concrete doorframes with glass brick surrounds. The front parlour was reinforced to double as an air-raid shelter, so the front window was originally partly blocked.

Most of the estates have been heavily altered, and that at Newport demolished, but some original details survive in Whitchurch. Jellicoe also designed pairs of houses at nearby Rhiwbina, with the town planner T. Alwyn Lloyd, but all but one now has a pitched roof.

Elain Harwood

1943

Brownsway Cottages

Architect: Ministry of Health
Location: Riding Lane, Hildenborough, Kent

Building decent, low-cost homes in the countryside is an old issue, never more pressing than during the Second World War. The Minister of Health, Ernest Brown, promised 3,000 standard cottages for farmworkers digging for victory. They were to be ready by harvest time, but high costs and government bureaucracy caused delays. The first pair was built by Tonbridge Rural District Council in eleven weeks at Hildenborough, and opened on 15 September 1943 by Brown and members of the women's land army. The cottages 'of strictly practical aspect', according to *The Scotsman*, were of colour-washed brick painted yellow, with bright green doors; the Fletton bricks and concrete lintels are now exposed in all their austere sobriety. Later examples featured low entrances to the sides, alongside wash-houses, a plan popularised by Tayler and Green (see page 73) for Lothingland RDC, Suffolk (the most expensive cottages under the scheme) and widely built into the 1950s.

Elain Harwood

1944

BISF House

Architect: Frederick Gibberd
Location: Northolt, Middlesex

In 1943, the British Iron and Steel Federation (BISF) appointed Frederick Gibberd to design experimental prefabricated steel-framed houses as part of the Government's demonstration housing project in Middlesex. Two pairs of two-storey semi-detached BISF Houses were constructed among 13 experimental semis at Northolt, using a mixture of prefabricated and site-built elements. The upper storey of the lightweight structural steel frame was clad in profiled steel sheets, while the ground floor walls were clad in non-load-bearing brickwork.

Gibberd believed it important to introduce natural, traditional materials, such as brick, to soften the appearance of machine-made forms. Furthermore, he stressed that factory-made houses must be designed in relationship to the site and to one another – an indication of his growing interest in aesthetics and picturesque planning.

This came to be regarded as the only prefab with architectural merit and was the most widely used steel-framed house in post-war estates; several variants were designed and reproduced in large numbers.

Christine Hui Lan Manley

1945

Wake Green Road

Architect: Ministry of Works
Location: Moseley, Birmingham
Status: Listed Grade II

The Wake Green Road prefabs still stand proud more than 70 years since they were built as a temporary solution to Britain's post-war housing problems. Between 1944 and 1949, more than 156,000 two-bedroom temporary bungalows rose across the UK under the Temporary Housing Programme. Over 4,000 were in Birmingham: although they have been well-loved by the people who lived in them, most have been pulled down. All the bungalows had a minimum 635 sq ft (257sq m) floor space and were assembled from prebuilt panels attached to prefabricated wood or metal frames. The Wake Green Road houses are the Phoenix type – detached, three-bay, steel-framed and clad in corrugated asbestos sheeting with metal windows.

All prefabs came with a central service unit of a prefabricated kitchen built onto a bathroom and indoor lavatory with central service pipes and a coal fire and back boiler to fuel hot water and a hot air central heating system. The kitchens contained the latest labour-saving equipment and were luxurious for the time.

The Birmingham prefabs were listed grade II in 1998 as 'an unusual surviving example'. Birmingham Conservation Trust, the Twentieth Century Society in the West Midlands and the Prefab Museum are working on the Prefabulous project to conserve the bungalows, several of which are empty and in poor repair.

Lou Robson

New House

Architect: F.R.S. Yorke
Location: Luccombe, Shanklin, Isle of Wight

Immediately after 1945, private building was almost illegal. One way to get a licence was to demonstrate that the project was a trial of a technical innovation, as F.R.S. Yorke, a veteran of the 1930s Modern Movement in Britain, was able to do in respect of the concrete foundations for this holiday house for his own family. 'Opus One' of his new partnership with Eugene Rosenberg and Cyril Mardall, it is a simple bungalow, its elevation forming a frame with compartments. The 'random rubble' walling, traceable to Le Corbusier's pre-war influence, was also a feature of the temporary Gane Pavilion in Bristol of 1936 by Yorke's then partner, Marcel Breuer, which itself predicted the swing away from machine-finishes. The Yorkes left after a year and sold the house to the district nurse, Miss Triggs, who cherished it.

Alan Powers

1947

The Thistle Foundation

Architect: Stuart Matthew of Lorimer and Matthew
Location: Niddrie Mains Road, Edinburgh
Status: Listed Category B and Conservation Area

The commission for this pioneering housing estate was won by Stuart Matthew in a competition in 1945. The Foundation's creators, Sir Francis and Lady Tudsbery, sought to improve on long-term hospitalisation by introducing a new concept of care for severely wounded ex-servicemen. Necessary treatment was provided on-site while the recipients were able 'to live in homes of their own, surrounded by their own families, by their own friends, and by their own belongings.'

The terraced patio-plan houses were set around rectangular and fan-shaped courts. Substantial lawns interposed the groups served by integrated streetscape, a sweeping central corridor and linked with covered walkways to communal buildings. Distinct reference to traditional Scottish east-coast design was made in the pantiles, slates and gabled runs. The later, inter-denominational Robin Chapel formed a centrepiece. The range of housing types responded to the special needs of the tenants and resulted in a remarkable village-like complex without precedent in the UK.

Deborah Mays

1948

1–4 Walker Terrace

Architect: Peter Dunham
Location: Asthall, Oxfordshire

Samuel Walker began farming in Asthall when in 1927–28 he bought land from the Mitford's estate. In 1947, he gave a site in the hamlet to Witney Rural District Council for a terrace of four cottages on condition that one could be reserved for his workers. The result was Walker Terrace: the first new housing there for nearly a century and carefully built using local stone to fit with the adjoining cottages. Although terraced, the houses somewhat resembled the cottages at Hildenborough in Kent (see page 65), with three bedrooms, a large living room and downstairs lavatory as well as an upstairs bathroom. It secured the most votes of any nomination for a Festival of Britain merit award (equally with Newbury Park bus station), and uniquely the plaque is also stone-coloured.

Peter Dunham trained under Albert Richardson and had a small practice based in Luton and his native Dunstable, mainly designing housing.

Elain Harwood

1949

20 Forthlin Road

Architect: Liverpool City Council Architect's Department
Location: Liverpool, Merseyside
Status: Listed Grade II

The listing of this modest, suburban post-war council house, in a terrace of eight, might be baffling until one remembers that the listing criteria include special historic interest and that (Sir) Paul McCartney (b.1942) lived at 20 Forthlin Road from the ages of 13–22.

McCartney's family was supportive of his extraordinary songwriting talent and up to 100 Beatles songs were composed within its unassuming walls. This small house bore witness to his early musical apprenticeship with John Lennon, who lived nearby at the semi-detached Mendips, and both houses were places of intense creativity and musical production.

Not many original fittings survive, save the linoleum in McCartney's bedroom, but the National Trust has evocatively restored the house to its early post-war appearance. While clearly possessing historic associations of international proportions, it is a serendipitous outcome that the most ordinary of post-war English houses is now captured for posterity on the National Heritage List.

Emily Gee

1950

Maes Hyfryd/Bryn Teg

Architect: Sidney Colwyn Foulkes
Location: Beaumaris, Anglesey

It is refreshing to see housing that is of its time and does not hanker after the past in nostalgic detail. Built in 1950, this estate is modern yet not regimented. Indeed, the terraces sit comfortably on the hillside above Beaumaris, sometimes stepping down the slope, sometimes following the contours. Often the terraces terminate with a gabled house, like a bookend.

Foulkes took great pains with the layout, providing green spaces and wide verges, and views of the sea and mountains beyond. He planned the houses with care, too, choosing terraces in preference to the usual semi-detached format. The houses have wide frontages, maximising view and sunlight, and horizontal windows (originally modernist metal casements). Colwyn Foulkes, who came from a family of builders and developers and was a joiner by training, flouted the building byelaws by lowering the ceiling heights but when Aneurin Bevan visited, he deemed 7ft 6in (2.3m) was quite acceptable, and this later became the national standard.

Adam Voelcker

1951

The Woodyard Square

Architect: Herbert Tayler and David Green
Location: Woodton, Norfolk

Between 1947 and 1973, Herbert Tayler and David Green built council houses in some two dozen villages in the Loddon Rural District. At a time when such housing tended to look perfunctory and out of place, Tayler and Green composed with the lie of the flattish terrain, thinking about landscape as a modelling of space. They were picturesque in the eighteenth-century sense, evoking local character, inviting exploration through surprises, and not afraid of prettiness. As early as 1962 Pevsner called them 'post-modern', for they didn't think flat roofs suited the place or the people.

The Woodyard Square enjoys a hillside, with a two-storey terrace ascending one side in steps, and single-storey old people's bungalows coming down the other, framing a triangle of grass where daffodils grow under the beech trees in spring. The sky is caught in the gap between them.

Alan Powers

1952

Garden Ground

Architect: Robert Townsend
Location: Bulford Road, Durrington, Wiltshire
Status: Listed Grade II

Robert Townsend claimed to be Frank Lloyd Wright's first British fan, writing an article on him in 1949 and organising Britain's first comprehensive exhibition in 1959. He believed Wright's houses reflected man's soul, with 'yin and yang', and they inspired his use of stone or – as here – earthy red brick, which he combined with timber in a translation of the Usonian house to Wessex.

Townsend built Garden Ground for himself and his wife, a doctor whose surgery and dispensary occupied the front part of the house. The centrepiece is a double-height living area set diagonally to the other rooms, a feature of all Townsend's most ambitious houses. The interior is dominated by timber: hardwoods in the living room and kitchen with plywood elsewhere, including boarded roofs and built-in cupboards and shelving.

In the 1960s Townsend turned to church work and became a deacon of the Roman Catholic church.

Elain Harwood

1953

Mardyke Road

Architect: Frederick Gibberd in collaboration with the Harlow
Development Corporation [HDC] Design Group
Location: 3–12 & 161–5 Mardyke Road, Orchard Croft, Harlow, Essex
Status: Listed Grade II

Orchard Croft forms part of Harlow's Mark Hall South neighbourhood. Gibberd's desire for higher residential densities, coupled with an increase in the town's target population, led to the revised Harlow master plan of 1952. Mark Hall South was planned to 50, rather than 38, persons per acre, (0.4ha) giving Gibberd the opportunity to introduce more urban housing.

At Mardyke Road, he designed an impressive crescent of three-storey terraced houses overlooking a cricket field at the southern extent of Orchard Croft. Constructed in brown brick, rendered at ground floor level and with projecting concrete surrounds to first-floor windows, the terrace forms a definite urban edge in contrast to the adjacent open space – a composition inspired by the 1790s Fortfield Terrace at Sidmouth, Devon. It signifies Gibberd's ambition to create a sense of urbanity at Harlow and marks a clear progression from the low density 'prairie planning' of earlier neighbourhoods.

Christine Hui Lan Manley

1954

Martin's

Architect: Powell and Moya
Location: Scords Lane, Toy's Hill, Brasted, Kent
Status: Listed Grade II

Powell and Moya's private houses are not well known, and most have been demolished. The exception is the finest, built for Monica and Muriel Anthony, spinster sisters who wanted a weekend retreat and who were recommended to these up-and-coming architects by Monica's friend Ian McCallum of the *Architectural Review*. Licensing restricted building materials, but the disjointed profile and fine internal finishes make Martin's a striking piece of late constructivism.

The site slopes steeply. A garage and box room were built on the road front, dignified by cedar boarding. The rest of the house comprises two linked single-storey pavilions set down the hillside. One houses the large living area, given added height by being placed lower than the dining room and kitchen under a common flat roof. Built-in bookcases resemble those in Powell's own house. The bedroom wing gave each sister a room with a view.

Elain Harwood

1955

The Goddard House

Architect: Fello Atkinson and Brenda Walker:
James Cubitt and Partners
Location: 22 Avenue Road, Leicester
Status: Listed Grade II

In 1953 Herald and Joan Goddard commissioned
Atkinson (partner) and Walker (job architect) to
design their 'ideal home'. The Goddards were
interested in Bauhaus architecture, indoor-outdoor
living, and Frank Lloyd Wright's open-plan interiors,
while Atkinson had recently seen light-filled
modernist homes (including 'Case Study' ones) in
the United States.

These aesthetic preferences, plus the post-war
restriction on domestic houses to 1,500sq ft (139.4sq
m), resulted in an L-shaped single-storey house of
white Cambridgeshire brick with timber fascia, and
glass walls, using the largest double-glazed units
then available, overlooking and giving access to the
garden. The frame was 'Benfix' timber with light
steel joists and 2in thermacoustic panels. Other
'modern' features included an open-plan dining-
living-study area, children's wing with playroom,
an integral garage, and underfloor central heating.
Materials were restricted but sufficient local and
Empire materials were found, from African muhuhu
wood for the main floor to Westmorland slate for the
hearth on the brick fireplace wall.

Pat Kirkham

Labour-saving homes: The impact of domestic technology

Kathryn Ferry

During the twentieth century the way British homes were run changed dramatically. In 1901 the routine tasks of heating, lighting, cooking, cleaning and washing were frequently undertaken by servants; even lower-middle-class clerks could expect to employ a maid and that year's census showed ten per cent of women over the age of ten worked in domestic service. By the mid-twentieth century the principal aid to domestic life was electricity, powering a multitude of household appliances. The key transformative period spanned the late 1950s and early 1960s when wartime innovations made it into the home and full employment allowed for the purchase of new labour-saving technology. Nowhere was this more apparent than in the kitchen which developed from a functional back-stairs area of the house into the heart of the modern home.

Domestic architecture reflected these social and technological changes. In Victorian houses built to be shared with paid staff, internal space was typically zoned with the servants' domain centred on the kitchen and its ancillary 'offices' of larder, scullery and coal store. As long as there was a ready supply of cheap labour the incentive for improving these utilitarian spaces was strictly limited. The impetus came after the First World War when women leaving the munitions factories chose overwhelmingly *not* to return to the drudgery of domestic service. The previously leisured ladies of the middle classes now found themselves running their own homes and the inadeqaucy of the tools at their disposal came sharply into focus. Commodities and dwellings marketed as 'labour-saving' thus became increasingly desirable from the 1920s and 1930s. Over the ensuing decades, as the kitchen was fully integrated into the house, the larder, scullery and coal store

gradually disappeared from achitects' plans. Food storage was shared between a refrigerator and the modular units of fitted kitchens; wet jobs once confined to the scullery could be done at the plumbed-in kitchen sink while weekly laundry was done in a fraction of the time thanks to the automatic washing machine; the old coal-hungry range gave way to a more compact oven and the task of heating water and rooms was given over to a central heating boiler. In their use of space and labour all of these replacements could claim greater efficiency over their predecessors.

By 1914 the everyday household appliances we take for granted were already in existence, however their high cost and the lack of widespread power supply confirmed them as luxuries for the rich. In 1918 just 6 per cent of homes were wired for electricity. Mass acquisition of home gadgetry required mass connection and in 1926 the National Grid was set up to effect this change. Eighty per cent of homes were connected by 1946, 90 per cent by 1951 and the remainder brought in by the 1950s supergrid. As with any new technology there were early fears to overcome but as Sigfried Giedion observed in his 1945 study *Mechanisation Takes Command,* electricity '...meant to the mechanisation of the household what the wheel meant to moving loads'. Its potential for improving domestic life was fully embraced by the Electrical Association for Women, which was founded in 1924 and had more than 10,000 members in the 1950s. As well as organising meetings, surveys and cookery competitions, this organisation trained girls to work as demonstrators in electricity showrooms. Their task was vastly helped by the post-war launch of the three-pin plug and the standardisation of sockets to

Above Only top of the range washing machines featured immersion heaters in the 1950s but for £7–8 a gas wash-boiler like the one seen here could improve the drudgery of wash day, either in combination with an agitating machine or instead of one. Damp clothes were then passed through a manual wringer at the sink.

fit the new ring main circuits. Commenting on this innovation in 1956, *Good Housekeeping* noted that in houses built pre-war it was common to find 'anything up to ten different types of plug in use for your various domestic appliances – 2-pin, 3-pin, bayonet-cap, 2-amp, 5-amp, 10-amp, 15-amp...' Nearly every plug was looped back to its own individual fuse on the main fuseboard, meaning 'hundreds of yards of wiring in the smallest of houses', and dependence on adapters that would frequently overload the mains and put out the lights. Though the ring main conquered these difficulties capacity was still limited;

the average number of sockets for post-war new builds was just six *per house*.

Even with the nationwide provision of electricity the uptake of domestic technology remained gradual due to its expense. With the end of post-war austerity and the export drive necessary to boost economic recovery, social and manufacturing advances combined to make appliances highly aspirational and increasingly affordable. Not only was there full employment, the number of married women who stayed in the workplace rose from 18 per cent in 1947 to over 50 per cent in 1961. Advertisers

Above This 1957 kitchen was designed for the 'Silicone' show home at No.51 Northbrooks in Harlow New Town. It combined modern appliances including cooker, fridge, washing machine, water heater and even electric frying pan, with a bold contemporary wallpaper.

targeted those women who were earning money but were still expected to do the bulk of household chores with bright images and heady promises of lives made easier by technology. At the same time new materials such as aluminium, laminates and plastics, that had been tested during the war, became available for commercial purposes. Techniques of mass production were also applied to goods for the home massively broadening the range available.

The average post-war kitchen cooked around a thousand meals a year so it was hardly surprising that an oven was considered the most essential investment. Even figures for 1931 are testament

to this priority; by that date there were already 1.3 million electric cookers in British homes compared to just 400,000 vacuum cleaners, 220,000 refrigerators and a mere 60,000 washing machines. Between the wars refrigerators were huge and expensive. In 1922 *The Daily Mail Bungalow Book* carried an advert for the 'Freezone Food Cabinet' which assured would-be purchasers it would dispense with the need for larders and costly cellars. Such savings might be attractive to builders of bespoke bungalows, *the* labour-saving homes of the era, but the Freezone's 98-guinea price tag put it out of reach for most people. The generally cool

British climate did not impel purchase in the way it did in hot American states. There was also an urban/rural dimension with continued reliance on larders outside big cities even as 1950s marketing began to promote the fridge as a necessity of modern life. Proof that this American-inspired advertising copy was having an effect came in 1958 when the removal of purchase tax restrictions released a pent-up demand that saw annual refrigerator sales hit a record high of 440,000. By 1961 23 per cent of British households owned one, still a low figure but a substantial increase on the 3.5 per cent ownership found in 1953. Not until the mid-1980s did the fridge become a truly universal appliance. The same was true of washing machines. In the 1950s their automatic capabilities were actually quite limited; not being plumbed in, machines had to be moved over to the kitchen sink where they would then have to be emptied by hand following the power-driven 'agitation' of the clothes. Wet items were individually passed through a hand-turned wringer before drying. That these were the most sought-after of all labour-saving appliances says much for the back-breaking toil otherwise required for the weekly laundry.

As more technology was accepted into the domestic sphere the kitchen itself began to be perceived in a more scientific way. Evidence from an increasing number of time and motion studies showed how much labour a poorly-planned kitchen could waste. Researchers in the 1950s thus formulated an ideal 'triangle' between work surface, cooker and sink to reduce unnecessary footsteps. Unfortunately, the location of key fixtures was frequently beyond the housewife's control and even moving into a new home was no guarantee of an ideally planned kitchen. In 1953 the Building Research Station examined the efficiency of kitchens designed by Powell and Moya for local authority flats in the Churchill Gardens Estate in Pimlico, London. Testers not only claimed that a few simple changes in layout could reduce the distance occupants travelled by an average 18 per cent; they also managed to make space for a table and chairs to convert the working kitchenette into a more popular kitchen-dining room. This idea of multi-use spaces had a big impact on the way kitchens were integrated into the overall house plan. The social stigma that associated eating food in the same place as it was prepared with a lower class of residence was swept away by the fashion for open-planning and kitchens became much more informal spaces. The new fitted units available for mass consumption after the war

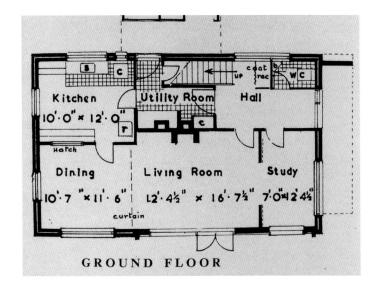

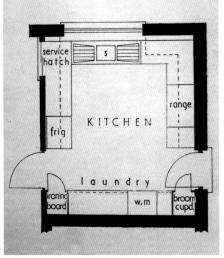

Above left A 1955 house plan demonstrates how rooms on the ground floor were becoming more integrated. A serving hatch connects the kitchen with the dining-living room, and the old-fashioned scullery is replaced by a utility room.

Above right An unbroken 'U' was promoted as the most practical arrangement for a well-planned kitchen with the sink, preferably under the window, at the mid-point of the work centres.

reflected this in the range of their vibrant colours and functions. Manufacturer Redwing promoted its fitted kitchen as a 'store-room, cafeteria, [and] nursery, all rolled into one!' It claimed to be both highly practical *and* cheerful, a combination that summed up the desires of a generation leaving the war years behind.

At the 1956 Ideal Home Exhibition architects Alison and Peter Smithson created a 'House of the Future' prophesising the huge impact changes in domestic technology would continue to have on British homes. From a point of post-war optimism they looked ahead to the early 1980s and foresaw electricity provided by the nearest atomic power station, dishwashers which disposed of all food waste, kitchen sinks made of glass-reinforced plastic, 'super high-frequency' ovens for cooking at high speed and electric saucepans made of non-stick titanium. That the majority of what they imagined has come to pass proves just how all-pervasive technology became in our homes, and in particular in our kitchens, over the course of the twentieth century.

Above The original kitchen by Alison Smithson survives in the house she and Peter designed for Derek and Jean Sugden, built in 1955–56. Derek Sugden (1924–2015) proudly claimed that in 60 years he only changed the boiler.

1956

Rushbrooke

Architect: John Weeks
Location: Rushbrooke, Suffolk
Status: Listed Grade II

After the Second World War, when the estate village might have seemed an anachronism, a small outcrop occurred near Bury St Edmunds. The Rothschild family bought the Rushbrooke Estate and Victor Rothschild turned to his old friend Richard Llewelyn-Davies for advice. John Weeks, his friend (and soon architectural partner in Llewelyn-Davies and Weeks) designed a hamlet of monopitch, slate-roofed and white-walled cottages, almost picturesque in their siting while unyieldingly modernist in detail. With crisp fenestration – on occasion leaving elevations virtually unbroken, elsewhere running generous clerestory lighting below the eaves – the cottages, for estate employees, have an urbanity that is hard to find outside the post-war new towns. Continuing in the original ownership until 2014, careful maintenance has preserved the hamlet. The first cottages, sited slightly apart (Poplar Meadow 1952–56), were followed by two further phases (1956–59 and 1960–63) lining either side of the village street, carefully asymmetrical, framing the Tudor brick well-head.

Gillian Darley

The Pediment

Architect: Raymond Erith
Location: Aynho, Northamptonshire
Status: Listed Grade II

The simple austere style of this building, with its emphasis on proportion and fine detailing, is characteristic of the work of the architect Raymond Erith and his belief in classicism as a living tradition with continuing relevance for the twentieth century. The Pediment was built for a Scottish solicitor, Elizabeth Watt, a discriminating collector of modern paintings and works of art and a keen and knowledgeable gardener. The layout, structures, gates and walls of the garden form an integral part of Erith's design and this small house, built with large ashlar blocks of Bath stone to increase its apparent size, is surrounded by a landscaped park in miniature.

The client continued until Erith's death in 1973 to commission garden ornaments and buildings, including a Doric temple summerhouse (1959) and the splendid Croquet Shed (1964, listed grade II), conceived as 'a piece of architecture' to be viewed on an axis from the house.

Lucy Archer

1958

High Sunderland

Architect: Peter Womersley
Location: Near Selkirk, Scottish Borders
Status: Listed Grade A

High Sunderland was commissioned by textile designer and manufacturer Bernat Klein. He chose Womersley after visiting newly built Farnley Hey, near Huddersfield.

A single storey, flat-roofed, rectilinear pavilion constructed from timber and glass, High Sunderland sits on a wooded ridge overlooking the Ettrick Valley. With its interplay of verticals and horizontals, enlivened by coloured glass panels, the façade resembles a three-dimensional Mondrian painting.

Designed for zoned activities, the interiors are arranged in two distinct halves opening onto courtyard terraces. One wing contains the living room and master bedroom, the other accommodation for children and guests. At the axis are the kitchen and dining room. The large open-plan living room provides a sensational centrepiece, condensing three rooms into one, with a study at one end, a library along one side and a spacious sunken seating well in the centre. An inspiring but practical environment for family life, High Sunderland has the wow factor and was ideal for entertaining clients and journalists.

Lesley Jackson

1959

6 Bacon's Lane

Architect: Leonard Manasseh and Partners
Location: Highgate, London
Status: Listed Grade II

Leonard Manasseh built this home for himself and his young family just as his practice began to take off in the late 1950s. A covenant on the site, which adjoins the northern border of Highgate Cemetery, restricted the height of the building to two storeys, but within its modest envelope Manasseh ingeniously planned a multi-level house that seems to spread out in all directions, and with a marble-paved, upper-floor drawing room that rises to his studio below the great dormer above. Manasseh used squares and golden sections throughout the house, the disciplined geometry contrasting with decorative elements such as the *in situ* concrete panel that faces the garden.

Manasseh lived and worked in the house almost up to his 100th birthday in 2016 and the result was a perfectly composed and decorated late twentieth-century interior, full of his paintings and collections of furniture and objects.

Timothy Brittain-Catlin

Cedarwood

Architect: Dewi-Prys Thomas and Gerald Beech
Location: Woolton, Liverpool
Status: Listed Grade II*

Cedarwood is situated in the leafy suburbs of south Liverpool, close to where John Lennon and Paul McCartney grew up. It caused a sensation when it was opened to the public in March 1960 as the '*Womans' Journal* House of the Year' and thousands of people visited in the following three months, to gaze at the prospect of open-plan living, reflecting pools, underfloor heating, extensive use of plate glass and all the latest mod-cons.

Behind the excitement and glamour was a house whose architecture demonstrated the thoughtful integration of a modern family lifestyle into a compact and carefully proportioned structure, which made innovative use of timber for glu-lam beams and interior finishes, as well as the external cladding that gave the house its name.

Cedarwood offered a glimpse of the future. It has also stood the test of time.

Neil Swanson

Keelson

Architect: Eric Sørensen
Location: Hills Avenue, Cambridge
Status: Listed Grade II

The Cambridge crystallographer Olga Kennard bought a plot in 1960 and in vain looked for a British architect. So she turned to her professional contacts in Denmark, whence the great physicist Niels Bohr responded, 'Sørensen and no one else!' Although Scandinavian influences were strong in post-war architecture, few foreign architects built in Britain in the 1950s and 1960s. Dr Kennard remains delighted with her decision.

Keelson is a single-storey house the width of the narrow site, and Sørensen made a U-shaped plan around a courtyard, with the kitchen and dining room to the front, bedrooms off a broad corridor and a large living area facing the rear garden. Its understated elegance owes much to its slender timber frame, which is infilled with white-painted brickwork to a carefully irregular pattern to the front and large areas of glass to the rear. Sørensen also suggested some of the Danish furniture.

Elain Harwood

1962

Baldwin's Hill

Architect: Katz and Vaughan (assistant Roger Balkwill)
Location: East Grinstead, East Sussex

Hidden amid Victorian shrubbery is a house that resembles a set for a Bond villain, with a conversation pit beneath a hyperbolic parabaloid roof, and a swimming pool that flows under the glass curtain wall. It was commissioned by Fred Kobler, Managing Director of Grand Metropolitan Hotels, with guest bedrooms designed according to the specification used by the company. Kobler's bedroom is reached off the large living room and has a whole padded leather wall behind the bed, concealing a safe. The exterior is notable for its enamel steel panels in shades of green and orange.

Warsaw-born Bronek Katz (1912–60) moved to England in 1936, working for Maxwell Fry and Walter Gropius, where he met Reginald Vaughan. They went into partnership in 1945, with Bata shoes among their clients. Katz and Vaughan did lots of hotels for Kobler. The fact that Katz was killed in a skiing accident sums up the lifestyle of architect and client, rather like the house.

Alan Powers

1963

Ferrum House

Architect: John S. Bonnington
Location: Harpenden, Hertfordshire
Status: Listed Grade II

A young architect building a modern house for his family was a familiar feature of the 1960s, but Ferrum House, featured in detail in the *House & Garden Book of Modern Houses and Conversions*, 1966, epitomises the genre with its blend of American and European modernist influences – Bonnington had seen Mies van der Rohe's Farnsworth House near Chicago. Severe in its geometry, the house has a quiet richness of surface materials – Portland stone for the ground floor extending to the garden terrace, pine panelling and a white mosaic floor in living areas raised up to overlook the garden. Always immaculate inside, it is a masterly exercise in 'less is more'.

Jack Bonnington trained at Newcastle and after a spell in the USA, joined the office of Basil Spence, working on the Civic Centre at Sunderland and Kensington Town Hall, before starting his own successful international practice.

Alan Powers

1964

New House

Architect: Stout and Litchfield
Location: Shipton-under-Wychwood, Oxfordshire
Status: Listed Grade II*, landscape registered Grade II*

To enter through the secluded doorway into the Japanese garden of New House is to enter a secret world, best known to viewers of Stanley Kubrick's 1971 film *A Clockwork Orange*.

The house was built as a weekend retreat for the barrister Milton Grundy, a friend of Litchfield's. Cotswold stone and pitched roofs were a planning requirement, and the architects looked at local farm buildings in developing a series of linked pavilions that broke down the house's components. The largest contains a kitchen and dining area designed for informal parties, and three others each contain a bedroom with its own bathroom, door and view over the water garden. Splaying the walls to make each unit a parallelogram created slightly canted roofs, striking in an era of flat roofs.

The garden was designed by Viacheslav Atroshenko after he and Grundy visited Kyoto's Ryoan-Ji garden and Venice. Atroshenko added a mural in 1971.

Elain Harwood

1965

3 Church Walk

Architect: H.T. and Elizabeth Cadbury Brown
Location: Aldeburgh, Suffolk
Status: Listed Grade II

This little single-storey house is distinguished, but modest. Hidden behind ordinary houses with walled gardens, mostly of red brick, the only parts that project upwards are the 'light funnels'. Building for themselves, the Cadbury Browns chose a local pinkish-grey brick from Marks Tey and unusually, a courtyard plan.

Internally, it is white walled, with ceiling-height doors and no skirtings or architraves, a minimalist heaven. Circulation space is kept to a minimum but allows different routes through the house, parts of which can be closed off. The fun comes with the windows. In the living room, rather than a long expanse of plate glass, one window juts out into the garden towards the principal view. The guest bedroom has a similar, smaller projection and the main bedroom a triangular one. The sitting room is given precedence and is sunk below the level of the garden but the ceiling flows continuously, reinforcing long views through the house.

Harriet Edgerley

1966

Cockaigne Housing Group

Architect: Phippen Randall Parkes
Location: The Ryde, Hatfield, Hertfordshire
Status: Listed Grade II

Cockaigne Housing Group is a collective whose members own their houses, but share a clubroom incorporating a flat for visitors, a linear garden and a tennis court. On a long narrow site, there are 28 single dwellings, a mixture of one, two, three and four-bedroom single-storey terrace houses with flat timber roofs flanked by parallel concrete block party walls that extend to form private walled gardens.

Being on one level, the houses are easily adaptable to changing needs, and by retracting sliding partitions, children's bedrooms can extend the living space, or be used as studies and work rooms, once their occupants have left home.

A glazed internal patio and windows set in the roof bring sun and daylight to the heart of the larger houses, giving a spacious feel, while retaining privacy. Forming a close-knit community, these reassuring houses show that people on modest incomes can have access to high quality homes through co-operative endeavour.

Philip Hodgkinson

1967

Creekvean

Architect: Team 4
Location: Feock, Cornwall
Status: Listed Grade II*

The first built work of Norman Foster and Richard Rogers, partners in Team 4 from 1963–67, Creekvean seems at first sight to belong in California rather than Cornwall. The influence of the USA was pervasive: the pair had just returned from Yale, where Paul Rudolph was head of the architecture school and Serge Chermayeff a charismatic tutor. Their influence can be read at Creekvean, as can that of Frank Lloyd Wright, whom Rogers was later to regard as 'my first god'. Foster once told me that Johnson Wax was the most inspirational building he had ever seen.

The house took four tortuous years to build, but the clients, Rogers's then parents-in-law, Marcus and Rene Brumwell, were patient and Creekvean became a much-loved family retreat. Mrs Brumwell lived in the house until her death, in 2001 at the age of 99, still complaining of the draughts from the spectacular expanses of frameless glazing.

Kenneth Powell

1968

Trees

Architect: Ryder and Yates
Location: Middle Drive, Woolsington, Northumberland
Status: Listed Grade II

Trees, the first of two houses designed for the Ryder family, demonstrates recurring themes in plan, form and materials, which characterised their work. Built on a comparatively flat site, Trees is designed to exploit classic Northumberland views across farmland. The arrangement within a two-storey 'shoebox' form provides for family and guest accommodation with an area for entertaining. The main entry, midway along, uses a 'spatial valve' to link the entrance hall with the rooms it serves.

A duplex living area, with a Peter Yates mural, is contained in one volume with a ceiling formed of two parabolic sections, one concave and the other convex, highlighted by the glazed gable wall to the duplex. The first floor incorporates a balcony, the master bedroom with enclosed roof garden and guest accommodation. Independent accommodation for Ryder's four children is achieved via individual study bedrooms and a sitting room contained within a wing relating to the garden.

Rutter Carroll

New Ash Green

Architect: Eric Lyons, Span
Location: New Ash Green, Kent

Span developments had been around, and much admired, for some time when their architect Eric Lyons and his colleagues aired the ambitious project to develop a town in Kent. Buying two farms in 1961, the site would offer an entirely new version of a village. The Greater London Council (GLC) committed to take 450 houses, introducing mixed tenure and a more representative demographic than the professional middle class of Span developments. Two neighbourhoods were built (1966–69) and the shopping centre begun. Then, like a house of cards, the ambitious, idealistic project unravelled – the GLC pulled out, followed by Lyons, mortgages became scarce and funds ran out for the developers. Bovis stepped in and, in John Newman's words, 'the sparkle went out of the architecture'. At best, their elegant low-key modernism, embraced by its well treed landscape suggested to John Grindrod in *Concretopia* a place rather 'more like the setting for a Lars von Trier film than hop-growing country'.

Gillian Darley

1970

Capel Manor House

Architect: Michael Manser
Location: Horsmonden, Tonbridge, Kent
Status: Listed Grade II*

Capel Manor was a nineteenth-century Italianate Gothic house demolished in 1969, leaving a basement, a bank of steps and a deserted orangery. Manser placed his steel and glass structure on the axis of the steps on top of the basement adjoining the orangery.

The structure comprises four rectangular steel section tubes set into a concrete podium which sits on the stone walls of the earlier house; the steel frame is revealed both internally and externally while the roof overhangs the glazed façade. The lightness of the architecture is enhanced by the mullion-less corners.

It is Manser's most accomplished work in a series of houses he designed in the 1960s and 1970s. He developed the Miesian form to enclose comfortable family homes where the detailing became increasingly sophisticated as glazing and heating and ventilating technology developed.

Peter Murray

1971

Anderton House

Architect: Aldington and Craig
Location: Goodleigh, Devon
Status: Listed Grade II*

Mr Anderton was a family friend of Peter Aldington's, a pharmacist from Preston with a love of gardening who moved to work in Barnstaple. John Craig had recently moved out of advertising to join Aldington as a partner and he exercised a special skill in listening to the clients' description of how they wanted to live as a guide to Peter's design. Mrs Anderton hated her husband spreading paperwork across the living room and wanted him to have a separate study. He didn't want to shut himself away, and Peter found the answer: a solid enclosure between the kitchen and living room where the room steps down, high enough to hide the mess but low enough to see out. The timber frame was prefabricated for precision, and the rest of the simple structure completed beneath the sloping roof by local builders.

Beautiful and thoughtful, this house was bought by the Landmark Trust in the early 2000s and you can rent it for a holiday.

Alan Powers

Hill House

Architect: Denys Lasdun
Location: Near Headley, Hampshire
Status: Listed Grade II*

Hill House was designed by Denys Lasdun for Timothy Sainsbury as a country house and the home of much of his distinguished collection of art. The house stands atop a gentle hill in Arcadian countryside, and Lasdun and his client spent time considering and discussing the siting of the house to maximise the pleasure of the views, which are carefully framed by the house's windows.

The materials of the house are dominated by concrete: near-white 'forticrete' blockwork and board-marked *in situ*, which Lasdun was using at the same time on the National Theatre. This tough palette caused local rumours that a new school or military facility was being built, but in fact the generous spaces and beautiful craft quality of the construction make the interiors more reminiscent of the stone halls of ancient aristocracies than of post-war institutional architecture. Later additions track Lasdun's fascinating 1980s–90s stylistic development, with hints of Mackintosh and post-modernism.

Barnabas Calder

29½ Lansdowne Crescent

Architect: Jeremy Lever
Location: Lansdowne Crescent, London
Status: Listed Grade II

The site was difficult, a wedge-shaped gap between two houses with a width of 12¾ft (3.9m) at the front and 19½ft (6m) at the rear – narrower than the standard 22ft (6.7m) frontage elsewhere in the crescent, and sloping by 4ft (1.2m) from front to back. The aim was to have a basement flat of one-and-a-half floors that could be let or sold with the rest as a family home. This became seven floors to the rear and six floors at the front. Planning permission required a garage for two cars. In the course of building, it was found that the party walls leaned in by 6in (15.2cm) but much more serious was the contractor's mistake that led to the foundations and some of the lower structure being 35in (89cm) too high, calling for adjustments in heights throughout. All ended well however and brought an RIBA award that rightly commended the architect for 'courage, invention and skill'.

Jill Lever

Underhill

Architect: Arthur Quarmby
Location: Holme, West Yorkshire

This remarkable earth-sheltered house built around an indoor swimming pool was designed by Arthur Quarmby for himself and his family, who lived there for 40 years. Subterranean housing had been popular in America for a time, but Quarmby was the first for thousands of years to make use of the technique in Britain. The house is cut 16ft (5m) deep into the rock and wrapped with a light insulating skin. The result is a thermally efficient building which produces its own stable internal climate, and the undulating grass roof means that it has as little visual impact on its environment as it does ecologically.

Nestled high up in the West Yorkshire Moors where the family have lived for generations, Arthur Quarmby still retains the title of Constable of the Graveship of Holme, which allows him to collect turf from the moors to burn on his peat fire.

Tess Pinto

Eaglestone

Architect: Ralph Erskine, with Michael Andrews of Andrews, Sherlock and Partners
Location: Milton Keynes, Buckinghamshire

The English architect Ralph Erskine settled in Sweden in 1939 but found work drying up in the 1960s. A planning scheme for Cambridge University led to work at Clare Hall and for Bovis at Newmarket, who then asked that he collaborate in a competition for Eaglestone, one of the first grid squares of Milton Keynes developed privately.

Erskine planned 800 houses, of which only 324 were built, for sale and rent. Located on a slight hill, he grouped houses in tight village clusters around children's play areas, threaded by narrow paths either side of a central green and shopping precinct. The houses have the restless vitality distinctive to Erskine, brick walls contrasted with timber gables and eaves of varied colours, angled staircase windows and porches like those by him at Byker, Newcastle upon Tyne. Built to similar budgets as council housing in Milton Keynes, the neighbourhood has worn far better.

Elain Harwood

1976

Hopkins House

Architect: Michael and Patty Hopkins
Location: Hampstead, London

In 1975 two London architects designed the ideal building for themselves, their three young children and their growing architectural practice. Buying a site in Hampstead they evolved what they described as 'a rational and economical steel and glass construction', adapting technologies from industrial architecture.

The long, low building is constructed on a modular grid with light metal components, lattice trusses and steel columns giving an impression of floating in space. The approach to the house is over a steel footbridge. From the street-level first floor, originally the Hopkins's office, a spiral staircase leads down to the welcoming open-plan living space below.

The house had (and still retains) considerable shock value in its relatively staid Hampstead neighbourhood of Georgian and Regency architecture. It heralded new ideas of architectural structure based on lightness, transparency and adaptability, and provided an early and alluring demonstration of the flexible life-work patterns of the coming era.

Viewed across the street at night the Hopkins House still catches the attention as a shimmering symbol of twentieth-century modernity.

Fiona McCarthy

1977

Watermeads

Architect: R. Hodge and A. Bews: Merton Borough
Architects Department
Location: Rawnsley Avenue, Mitcham, Merton

Leslie Martin quickly established theoretical research
within the Architecture Department of Cambridge
University, where he and Lionel March devised
snaking low-rise terraces of houses that rivalled the
density of tower block estates. Cars were restricted
to one side of the housing, freeing the other for
pedestrian pathways and open space.

Among Martin's finest graduates was Richard
MacCormac, who expanded these studies when in
1967 he joined a new architects department at Merton.
His pioneer development was Pollards Hill in 1968–71,
before he left to build a snake of 4,000 houses in
private practice at Dyffryn, Newport. His remaining
colleagues at Merton built the finest exemplar of the
genre, however, at Watermeads in the mature grounds
of Mitcham Grove overlooking the River Wandle and
Ravensbury Park. There has been horrific window
replacement, but many originals survive – brown-
stained timber contrasting with beige panels, a severe
and ethical modernism.

Elain Harwood

1978

Branch Hill Estate

Architect: Gordon Benson and Alan Forsyth: Camden Architects Department
Location: Spedan Close, Hampstead, London
Status: Listed Grade II

Branch Hill was public housing's swansong. Its site in leafy middle-class Hampstead was challenging, constrained by covenants restricting development to two-storey semi-detached houses. Neave Brown had pioneered building low-rise housing at high densities in Camden, but Benson and Forsyth explored a third dimension by pushing elements backwards as well as up.

The flat roof of each house is the terrace of the next one up the hillside, reached by external walkways and steel stairs that lead to a first-floor kitchen and living area over ground-floor bedrooms. The structural concrete skeleton is board-marked and chamfered, and smooth infill panels are dazzlingly white. None of this came cheap and Conservative councillors tried to stop it, but the *Architects' Journal* considered it 'some of the highest quality council accommodation in the country'. The shame is that there was no more, for Margaret Thatcher triumphed for the Conservatives in 1979 and ended council building.

Elain Harwood

St Mark's Road Housing

Architect: Jeremy and Fenella Dixon
Location: North Kensington, London

With this pioneering project Jeremy Dixon acknowledged the crisis of modernism by rediscovering the language of London's terraces and streets. What appears to be a row of stately townhouses is in fact pairs of narrow-fronted houses over flats. Steps up and down give access to front doors and a place to linger and chat. Less typical is the way in which the plans are cranked to squeeze more leg-room out of the shallow plot.

An eclectic gathering of motifs – crowstepped gables, round-arched windows, a Mondrian gridded porch – comes together to present a cheery face to its Victorian neighbours. The pyramidal gateposts are a wry nod back to Jeremy and Fenella Dixon's competition entry for Northamptonshire County Hall. Related are the Dixons' Lanark Road (1981–83) and Ashmill Street (1983–85) in Maida Vale, and Compass Point (1984–87) on the Isle of Dogs.

Geraint Franklin

1980

Segal Close

Architect: Walter Segal
Location: Lewisham, London

A cul-de-sac in Lewisham is the site for the first part of a brave, and sadly unparalleled, adventure in local authority housing provision. In the late 1970s, Nicholas Taylor, Lewisham Labour councillor and architectural historian, and Walter Segal, an independently minded Swiss-born architect, saw the possibilities in an awkward pocket of council owned hilly ground. People were encouraged to plunge in and build their own homes, applying Segal's simple timber-framed system, which required little more than the ability to bolt the structural members together and infill them with lightweight panels. Plenty of guidance and support were on offer and the project took off. Despite divergent tastes in matters of detail, especially interiors, the group completed their houses to a common standard and the cooperative exercise also cemented a sense of shared endeavour and achievement. A second phase was added after Segal's death. The Walter Segal Self Build Trust keeps the flag flying while Segal's names adorn two of the streets he brought into being.

Gillian Darley

Noak Bridge

Architect: Maurice Naunton and George Garrard
Location: Noak Bridge, Basildon, Essex

Most people have heard of Poundbury, but few have heard of Noak Bridge, an extension of Basildon New Town designed by architects within the development who, after toeing the rationalist line for many years, thought 'why don't we design a place we would like to live in ourselves?'

The brief was similar to Poundbury, based on the realisation that the widths dictated by road engineers, combined with on-street or front garden parking, had destroyed the intimacy and enclosure cherished in historic settlements. The alternatives were simple in principle – parking at the back of groups of houses, and use of curved streets to avoid overlooking, but each part of the site required detailed thinking. The historic styles of the houses also anticipate Poundbury, and were introduced partly for variety and partly because people liked them. When the first were offered on the open market instead of rental, aspirant buyers queued up round the block.

Alan Powers

1982

Eagle Rock House

Architect: Ian Ritchie Architects
Location: Coopers Green, Uckfield, East Sussex

My first impression of Eagle Rock house was that it was lightweight, insubstantial, even temporary. But at the same time I was intrigued. The more I investigated, the more I realised that this is actually an incredibly strong design created to make a statement. The large planes of glazing and lightweight steel structure allow the building to blend into its background and the transitions between inside and outside space to become gentle and natural. The original concept of a bird can be seen not only in the overall plan form and volumes of the building but in the way it is camouflaged in its woodland setting. The architect has used the bird metaphor to the last detail: even the external blinds represent feathers, their movement described by the architect as being ruffled in the breeze. This attention to detail was recognised by the award of the *Architectural Design* Silver Medal in 1983.

Clare Price

Greenbank House

Architect: James Gowan
Location: 8 Greenbank, off Eaton Road, Chester

This is the second house that Gowan built for furniture designer Chaim Schreiber; the first was near Hampstead Heath (1964). Its high pitched roof draws the familiar symbol for 'house'. But that homely shape is subverted by the big circular porthole punched through a triangular gable that is boldly cantilevered out over the terrace. The huge roof almost hovers above the run of full-height glazing around the ground floor, but is supported on pilotis, in what Gowan considered a subversion of Le Corbusier as his work assumed post-modernist elements.

All the main accommodation is on the ground floor – living and dining area, study and master bedroom, plus a kitchen with its own service entrance. The roof accommodates guests and boiler room, lit by two clerestory windows in the ridge. The interior is beautifully detailed with architraves made to match the skirting and bespoke cabinetry as befitted Schreiber's reputation, but illness meant that he never lived there.

Susannah Charlton

1984

Yacht House

Architect: Richard Horden
Location: New Forest, Hampshire

London architect Richard Horden worked with Norman Foster as an associate for ten years into the mid-1980s when he established his own practice. He is a keen sailor with an interest in lightweight structures.

His first full-scale exploration of aluminum in domestic architecture was the Yacht House of 1984, erected in the New Forest for a private client. The house was named because it was built utilising as the principal structural elements the aluminium spars and masts used to fit out a Tornado yacht. After the concrete slab was laid by a local builder the aluminium and stainless steel frame was assembled onsite by the owner and family in just over five hours.

The house is a perfect square on plan of 5 x 5 structural bays with a centrally located entrance. The predominantly horizontal architecture nestles comfortably into the woodland providing dramatic views over the Avon river valley.

Don Gray

1985

Barley Splatt

Architect: Graham and Annie Ovenden with Martin Johnson
Location: Bodmin, Cornwall

Barley Splatt is not easily categorised: it is not so much post-modern as an extraordinary example of Gothic Revival Revival. It is an imaginative architectural expression of the growing, serious interest in Victorian Gothic encouraged by John Betjeman and by the success of the Victorian Society in the 1960s. The house was the creation of the controversial artist and historian of photography, Graham Ovenden, and his artist wife Annie, both members of the Brotherhood of Ruralists, working with the architect Martin Johnson. Having moved to Cornwall, the couple bought a cottage in 1974 and enlarged it over the following decade (although it remains unfinished). There are references to the work of such great Victorians as Augustus Pugin and William Burges, multi-coloured tiles on the roofs and structural polychromy in the rugged stone walls. The rich, dense interiors incorporate recycled material from, amongst other buildings, G.E. Street's convent at East Grinstead and tiles by Pugin, while many witty details, like the stylised crossbows on the exterior walls, were Ovenden's own invention.

Rosemary Hill and Gavin Stamp

Wadhurst Park

Architect: John Outram
Location: Wadhurst, East Sussex

Hans Rausing, co-owner of Tetra Pak, settled at Wadhurst to avoid Swedish tax and breed deer, and promised his wife Märit a house. Their landscape designer Anthony du Gard Pasley introduced Outram, who built alongside a ruined conservatory surviving from an earlier Victorian house. 'It had to look established and not stupidly novel, rather solid, cultured and proper, yet original', he recalled.

The tall single storey acknowledges Rausing's 6ft 7in (2m) height. The plan evolved into an 'H' on an expressed 3ft/900mm grid, with a dark entrance hall serving a bright central saloon and an enfilade of rooms overlooking parkland. Its sources are Louis Kahn's Kimbell Museum and the flat façades of Outram's first warehouse at Poyle, Surrey. The steel frame is clad in brick and travertine, with piers of Outram's polychromatic 'blitzcrete' concrete (also used in a tiny Millennium Pavilion), and internally lined in marble and timber. The conservatory was roofed over in 1988.

Elain Harwood

Janet Street-Porter House

Architect: Campbell, Zoglovitch, Wilkinson and Gough
Location: Brittain Street, Clerkenwell, London

Janet Street-Porter and Piers Gough were contemporaries at the Architectural Association in the 1960s. She went on to pioneer 'youff TV'; he called what he did 'B-movie architecture'. At this Clerkenwell house they were reunited as client and architect: the perfect Po-Mo pairing.

The result is spiky and tough; deliberately uninviting yet curiously endearing. The brickwork becomes progressively darker towards the pavement (creating a *trompe-l'oeil* shadow effect) and the lintels are concrete tree trunks, while sloping sills and diamond glazing transmogrify into a trellis grid, which alarmingly shoots away from its corner site. A helm roof clad in aquamarine pantiles encloses a penthouse studio.

Inside, raw surfaces and 'as found' elements sidle up to handcrafted finishes. Each room has a different shape and decorative scheme, reflecting the restless camerawork and ticker-tape visuals of her TV shows. 'If you were asked "Who might this building belong to"', said Piers, 'I think you'd guess it was Janet.'

Geraint Franklin

'Now, building your house can be ever such fun': the architect and the patron

Alan Powers

The 100 years following 1914, despite the interruptions of war, has been an extraordinary period for building one-off houses in Britain. The number built by architects for themselves, chiefly between 1955 and 1975, and again in more recent years, surpasses any other period, but it has also been a time when architects and patrons have worked together to create houses with distinctive individuality, despite the additional cost of building a one-off. Behind every house in this book, therefore, is a story of shared adventure which for most people is the largest single expenditure they will ever make. This produces a delicate relationship requiring firm handling by the architect while allowing for a dialogue. From time to time, the RIBA has issued advice literature for domestic clients urging them to use an architect rather than trusting a surveyor or builder. In one such book from 1963, the author, Derek Senior, reassured his readers that 'the more widely your notions of the good life differ from those that are cherished by the people who determine how speculative builders' customers shall live, the more worthwhile you will find it. And if your architect is really good you may well get a thumping bonus – the means to a better life than you had known was possible for you.'

In *The Honeywood File*, a fictional account of a private house commission published in 1929 by the architect H.B. Cresswell, we find the pitfalls of the process as well as its pleasures, with a pompous businessman and his feather-brained wife in the hands of a novice architect (James Spinlove) who must tactfully steer them away from the influence of their friends and chance acquaintances, calm their nerves, and cope with unexpected events on the site, of which there are many. Cresswell's authorial comments on

the art of letter writing are useful advice even in the time of emails, and reveal how an architect working for a private client carries greater responsibilities in proportion to rewards than in other areas of work. The difficulties of dealing with clients, involving many hours of negotiation, and the relatively low financial reward for designing small houses – since architects' fees are a fixed percentage of the cost of a building – put off many architects (such as Tayler and Green) from taking the unprofitable commissions.

Reading correspondence files for private house commissions in architects' archives frequently feels like reading *The Honeywood File*. Oliver Hill, one of the most popular architects of the interwar years, comes across as charming, slightly bullying and resistant to taking blame for anything that goes wrong. At Gayfere House, Westminster, 1930, he won his battle with the future Lady Mount Temple, coaxing her to accept a marble staircase, and writing, 'to me [our house] represents your portrait in marble and glass and steel. … it is a monument to your judgement.' A year later, however, she wrote to him asking for acoustic panels in the dining room as 'everybody hates having a meal in it', but they remained friends. At Joldwynds, Hill's first major experiment in modernism at Holmbury St Mary, it was perhaps unwise to take risks with the future Lord Chief Justice, Sir Wilfred Greene, as your client. The flat roofs leaked and the smooth white render crazed and fell off. Lady Greene complained that the drawing room chairs were so deep you could not sit in them, and that once he had supervised an elaborate photography session, Hill was never seen on-site again. They demanded reparations, sold the house and built another, this time by Margaret Lubetkin of Tecton, insisting on a pitched roof. At

Above The Staircase, Gayfere House, Westminster, by Oliver Hill for Mr and Mrs Wilfred Ashley, later Lord and Lady Mount Temple, 1929–31.

the end of his career, Hill fell out with his last client, Mrs Morris-Keating at Long Newnton Priory, but sent his great nephew, Simon Verity, on a peace-making mission disguised as the butcher's boy on a bicycle, bearing a bunch of flowers with a hand-printed verse that ran:

My dear Mrs Keating you do take some beating
Rejecting with scoffer the pearls that I proffer.
Now, building your house could be ever such fun,
Take me back to your heart, please, and I'll come
with a run.

Clients for modernist houses could be counted on to be eccentric. In 1931, Amyas Connell was visited in his London office by Sir Arthur Lowes Dickinson,

who had seen pictures of Connell's High and Over, at Amersham – the first large-scale homegrown modernist house. 'Young man, I am an old man.' Sir Arthur began, 'I do not want a house to live in, but one in which I can spend my few remaining years and then die in.' The White House, Haslemere, one of the most original concrete houses of the early 1930s was the outcome. Those who commissioned houses from Connell and his partners Basil Ward and Colin Lucas could expect a rough ride, not with their architect, but with the planning authorities. One of them, the solicitor Geoffrey Walford, was proud to print on the invitation to the house-warming party at 66 Frognal in Hampstead a quote from Sir Robert Tasker, MP, at a meeting of the London County Council, calling the house '…one of the greatest

Above The White House (also known as Alding, Pollard and New Farm), Haslemere, Surrey, designed by Amyas Connell and Basil Ward for Sir Arthur Lowes Dickinson, 1931–32.

pieces of vandalism ever perpetrated in London.' At the nearby Sun House, Frognal Way, Maxwell Fry's client, P.H. Goodbrook, 'a working sporting tailor with an Italian wife and a shop in Hanover Square', was exemplary: 'He set me a financial target and two pages of typescript saying exactly how they lived, working hard by day and entertaining friends in the evening, the whole outfit centred upon an old Scottish housekeeper.'

In the post-war decades, there were fewer architects who made their living from designing houses for family and friends, but some exceptional architects still found themselves a succession of clients and were able to use these jobs to explore new ideas without the constraints of the private sector. Raymond Erith was a classical architect of deep conviction, but set himself apart from more conventional neo-Georgians. One of the subtlest compliments from architect to client can be found at Bentley Farm, East Sussex, a house Erith enlarged

for Mr and Mrs Gerald Askew at the beginning and end of the 1960s as a base for their wildfowl collection. He responded to Mrs Askew's enthusiasm for France, but the Askews had discovered northern Italy and the rural sources of Palladianism shortly before the project began, both national characters being present in different elements of the house. In addition, there are two sets of stone gatepiers for the drive, one of which is square on plan, but rotated 45 degrees, thus becoming a rebus of the owner's name.

Records of architects' relationship with clients are patchy, although speaking to both sides has usually revealed a long-lasting mutual affection in which architects tend to retain a paternal (or less often maternal) pride and protectiveness towards their children. They will thus engage not only with their original client but with successive generations and with successive owners of houses as they are sold on. Rodney Gordon sold Turnpoint, the house he had built for himself in 1961, but continued to pay regular

Above Living room, Sun House, Frognal Way, Hampstead, by E. Maxwell Fry, 1935.

visits, much to the frustration of the new owners.

A client can be too insistent that he or she knows what they want, and they can also be too uncertain. This is where the architect must lure them into a solution that, in the best cases, offers something they recognise as the best solution but could not have arrived at on their own. For Peter Aldington and John Craig, this meant a long brief-taking process by Craig, lasting up to a year, in which he asked apparently inconsequential questions about lifestyle and personal preferences, before drawing up a document that the client could agree by signing it. This brief did not indicate numbers of rooms or sizes, but was a condensation of the interviews from which Peter Aldington could start work on a design. Joan Wedgwood was a client who started from a photo in a magazine at the hairdressers of an Aldington house where there was a special floor-level window for the cat to look out of. She and her husband wanted to downsize in Suffolk and

to live, as far as possible, in their garden. Having been through a lengthy briefing process, studied the contours and considered their prize pieces of Georgian furniture, John and Peter decided that a single-story house on a former tennis court, with rather regular rooms and high ceilings would best answer their needs. The Wedgwoods took a little time to accept the Miesian black steel box they were offered, but were grateful for the insight during many happy years' residence. For a miracle, the planning committee waved it through.

In conversation with Ellis Woodman, James Gowan recalled his relationship with Chaim Schreiber, the furniture manufacturer for whom he built two houses, first in Hampstead in 1964 (listed Grade II), and later in Chester. A mutual friend put them in touch, after saying that Gowan would do an initial scheme for nothing 'and if Mr Schrieber didn't like it then fine. So, I produced the scheme and he didn't like it a bit! But I discovered over the years that he would invariably chuck out the first design. … It wasn't a good start, but as it turned out, once he had exhausted you by getting you to do schemes he was really very fair-minded.'

John Outram had a similar experience working for Hans and Märit Rausing, who had bought an estate at Wadhurst, East Sussex, to escape Swedish tax laws and to breed deer. They commissioned Outram in 1978 and despite regular meetings nothing was decided for the next three years, until he began to think the house was a dream project that would never happen. Then Hans Rausing's father became seriously ill and the house had to be built quickly to avoid paying death duties in Sweden.

Young architects have always had a ready-made market in generous parents and other relatives but have generally been less able to build for their personal friends and contemporaries. Finding a site remains one of the chief constraints. Prejudice against modernism on the part of planners and local residents has remained a constant frustration, leading to a widespread compromise style, usually involving pitched roofs with clipped eaves or in some cases earth-sheltered dwellings like Hobbit houses, although classical houses have proliferated, mostly out of the public eye. The age profile of clients varies from young bankers with swollen bonuses and occasional Young British Artists, to silver-haired downsizers, who have sold their Victorian houses in London and can afford to build afresh in the country or in a secluded urban mews.

Above Zero fossil fuel energy maisonettes and studio apartments with workspaces at BedZED, Wallington, Surrey, by Bill Dunster Architects, commissioned by Peabody and Bioregional, built 2000–02.

Above Aldington and Craig, Wedgwood House (Ketelfield), Higham, Suffolk, 1975–78. Drawing by John Craig, 1979.

Burton House

Architect: Richard Burton of Ahrends, Burton and Koralek
Location: Lady Margaret Road, Kentish Town, London

Most architects' own homes are modest buildings erected early in their careers for young families. Richard and Mireille Burton built their house after their four children had left home, constructing three generous main spaces defined by classical proportions and a bold timber frame. I'm reminded of Louis Kahn but Burton's inspiration was Frank Lloyd Wright's House on the Mesa of 1932, down to a south-facing conservatory that maintains an equable temperature all year round. Burton was one of the first architects to embrace high insulation values and 'long life, loose fit, low energy', the mantra of the 1970s, which he followed in his public housing as well as here. A studio was added in 1990 and an annexe in 2002.

This is no modern minimalism. The house is filled with much-loved objects – Mireille is the daughter of the artist Jupp Dernbach and their eldest sons produced much of the furniture.

Elain Harwood

Above The conservatory at the Burton House.

1989

42 (and 44) Rochester Place

Architect: David Wild
Location: Camden, London

Wild designed his own house in 1976 and built it himself in 1980–83, concrete-framed on deep piles cantilevered from a load-bearing wall away from a difficult neighbour. The smooth concrete and glass-reinforced render relate to the 1840 terraces opposite. The deep plan is based around a dogleg stair, allowing the first-floor living room to be 1½-height with a cube at its heart, all on a 3ft/900mm grid, topped by a steel-roofed workroom inspired by the Eames House.

The filmmaker Patrick Uden acquired the adjoining plot and in 1986 commissioned a second house from Wild, wider and with a double-height living area and balcony over ground-floor bedrooms. Steel upper parts contrast with concrete below. Financial crisis meant that Uden sold on the scheme to Don Tindall, who eliminated a roof terrace and introduced richer finishes including marble and granite. When Tindall moved out in 1999, a delighted Uden moved in.

Elain Harwood

Knight House

Architect: David Chipperfield
Location: Richmond, London

This house-cum-studio for the fashion photographer Nick Knight marks Chipperfield's ascendancy and the return of minimalist abstraction to British architecture. The starting point was Knight's parents' Festival of Britain-era house, which was stripped down and layered up. The plan stakes out the parallel existences of family and studio; a svelte spiral stair, reserved for the models, recalls Victorian artists' studios.

Chipperfield's pristine architecture of shifting planes, white rendered surfaces and carefully-framed views recalls the work of Tadao Ando and the De Stijl movement. Like the white boxes of the 1930s, a suburban setting has emboldened the architect while prompting introversion; its arrival, too, was heralded by a bruising planning battle. In 1998–2001 a second building was added for Knight's growing family, to which it is joined with a translucent link.

Geraint Franklin

1991

Ashfold House

Architect: John Simpson
Location: Ashfold, East Sussex

Unlike the mainstream of post-war classicism in country houses, Ashfold avoids Palladian precedents and might pass for an early work of John Soane. It is smaller than it looks, and one of its skills is to compress a complex plan without being overcrowded, even allowing space for a spatially complex stair under a central lantern. The house was designed for the architect's parents, and he was given freedom to commission furniture to his own Regency-style designs to mix among antiques. During the period of construction, John Simpson became the most prominent exponent of classicism in the public eye with his alternative schemes for Paternoster Square, London, and the site now known as One London. His work has included Oxford and Cambridge college interiors and extensions, and the Queen's Gallery at Buckingham Palace. In retrospect, compared to these, Ashfold has an appealing simplicity.

Alan Powers

1992

Hall House

Architect: Proctor and Matthews
Location: Burnham Overy Staithe, Norfolk

Hall House – named after the client – is an early project from this London practice that has earned a reputation for excellence and innovation in housing design. It is in fact an L-shaped house, and owes a debt to Frank Lloyd Wright's essays in this typology. Its two wings shelter a paved courtyard whose outer edges are framed by the remnants of a mature garden. As with Wright, so Proctor and Matthews have resorted to local materials to face the hybrid structure (cavity work on the outside of the 'L', Douglas fir frame on the courtyard side). The house has something of a Jekyll and Hyde character: it 'fits in' on the outward facing sides, with external walls of flint cobbles with red brick quoins, so keeping the planners sweet, while on the courtyard side the flints are set in galvanised steel trays forming spandrel panels sandwiched between large-format windows: altogether more contemporary.

Gerald Adler

Clach Mhor

Architect: Roddy Langmuir of Edward Cullinan Architects
Location: Avielochan, Inverness-shire

Clach Mhor ('Great Stone') in the Cairngorms was designed by Roddy Langmuir for his father. Built into a hillside, the larger, upper floor accommodates bedrooms and an open-plan living area. Within, levels are varied, daylight and views are carefully controlled, there is much bespoke furniture, while an exposed vaulted ceiling reveals exquisitely detailed timbers.

The house is clearly contemporary, but suggests a strong historical sensibility, with hints of Arts and Crafts thinking. As in Lutyens's work, forms are repeated and transformed. The circular end of the living room recurs in a raised dining area; it also reappears in portholes, steps and holes in the living-room timbers. Meanwhile, the external harling and bold chimney suggest Scots vernacular; sleeping platforms within evoke traditional bothies. Finally, the curves and the portholes recall Gribloch, the 'modern Scots' country house designed by Basil Spence and William Kininmonth in the 1930s. The award-winning result is a richly evocative example of sensitive, contextual modernism.

Alistair Fair

1994

Malator

Architect: Future Systems
Location: Druidstone, near Haverfordwest,
Pembrokeshire

While High Tech architecture is generally seen as
a British movement, Jan Kaplický (1937–2009)
became fascinated by American technology in
Czechoslovakia. It was only when he was joined by
Amanda Levete that his firm Future Systems enjoyed
success, with the media centre at Lord's coinciding
with the segmental-shaped Malator.

Malator is a holiday home for socialist
campaigners Bob and Gill Marshall-Andrews, built
into the hillside above a ravine overlooking the sea. It
was prefabricated off-site and then packed with earth
on two sides and over the roof, leaving a curved
front using the latest glass technology bolted together
and a small glazed rear entrance. The interior is
surprisingly generous, its central living space with a
built-in sofa raised around a wood stove separated
from the bedrooms by two lime green bathroom
pods, one incorporating the kitchen.

And the view is remarkable.

Elain Harwood

1995

Beach House

Architect: John Winter
Location: Doggetts Lane, Happisburgh, Norfolk

John Winter worked hard and his summer holidays were a Spartan affair, spending August in North Norfolk. The venue was a ramshackle collection of structures including a converted chicken hutch and a Wendy house brought at the RHS Chelsea Flower Show. In 1990 John decided to build a new house, a simple structure from off-the-peg steel and aluminum profiled sheets, supported by a lightweight steel frame fabricated by North Walsham Tractors. All the materials were self-finished as in John's words, 'one does not go on holiday to repair and paint a house'. The new house contained a living-kitchen-dining room, with a sunken snug pit in the centre replete with a log burner. The interior was lined throughout with oak-faced plywood panelling to add a 'touch of luxury'. The structure was light and low, nestling into the sand dunes and sheltered from the ravages of the Arctic Shore, the only maintainance an annual hosing down to wash off the salt spray.

Jonathan Ellis-Miller

1996

Cullinan-Harbour House

Architects and clients: Dominic and Henrietta Cullinan and Ivan and Roxanne Harbour
Location: Truman's Road, Dalston, London

Hackney has become a byword for inventive one-off houses built on awkward plots. The Cullinan-Harbour house, constructed on a car lot, was a pioneer, courageously innovative in both design and construction.

Having purchased the plot together, Cullinan and Harbour decided on a single semi-attached house hugging, indeed overhanging, the street. The key to their design is the interlocking double helix staircase, of cantilevered precast steps within a concrete drum rising through all three storeys.

They also took on the challenge of constructing most of the scheme themselves. A builder laid the ground floor slab, but they, helped by family and friends, completed the rest, including designing the concrete shuttering. They used some steelwork, plus conventional timber floor joists and tall aluminium window mullions (offspring of those used by Harbour at the Rogers Partnership).

Now locally listed, this block remains: bolder in concept than most of its successors and bearing the marks of its carefully crafted creation.

Elizabeth Robinson

Banham Studio House

Architect: Jonathan Ellis-Miller
Location: Prickwillow, Cambridgeshire

The steel house that Jonathan Ellis-Miller built for the artist Mary Banham at Prickwillow, Cambridgeshire, complements well his own house on the adjacent plot completed six years earlier. While the first sits low on the ground, this one is raised with 9¾ft (3m) high ceilings providing a well-lit studio space and views across the fens towards Ely Cathedral. Set on a 13ft (4m) grid, the bolted steel structure cantilevers to support a raised access deck and suspended louvres. The plan revolves around the centrally positioned kitchen/bathroom core accessed, externally, from the raised carport. Passive solar gain warms the studio's concrete floor and the 129sq ft(12 sq m) bank of Braithwaite tanks, which operate as a Trombe wall. Hinged screen-walls can close off the small area around the fireplace to make a snug or provide privacy for the bedroom. 'The Style that Nearly…' of which Reyner Banham wrote in his book *Los Angeles: The Architecture of Four Ecologies* becomes reality in his widow's house.

Neil Jackson

The Priory

Architect: Rick Mather
Location: Hampstead, London

From the street The Priory looks like a simple two-storey white rendered box with a projecting entrance hall. It could be mistaken for one of Hampstead's 1930s modernist villas, to which it pays knowing homage. The glass balustrade of the roof terrace and the frameless corner window of the bedroom give the building away as much more recent. This house continued Mather's ground-breaking structural glass designs, including the Now & Zen restaurant and an All Glass Extension, and was shortlisted for the Stirling Prize.

Mather's love of 'deceptively simple exteriors with complex interiors' is to the fore with the three-storey rear elevation allowing the basement pool to connect to the garden while allowing reflections to dance around the house through the glass floor and staircase above. A generous rooflight fulfils the client's request to see the sky while lying in the pool. The volumetric complexity prefigures Mather's later, larger-scale work at the Ashmolean Museum in Oxford.

Matthew Wickens

1999

Winterbrook House

Architect: Ken Shuttleworth
Location: Lower Compton, Wiltshire

Inspired by the heady days of 1920s experimental European architecture, many architects aim for the visual purity of original but sharp white forms yet few achieve it. Ken Shuttleworth's house for his family, designed when he was still a partner of Norman Foster, pulled this off magnificently at Winterbrook House, a building of simple curved elevations but a complex section. The plan, described affectionately by the *Architectural Review* as resembling 'two croissants mating', placed one crescent not quite concentrically within another so that an irregular corridor between them separated the fully-glazed, east-facing open living area at the front from the top-lit cellular bedrooms and bathrooms behind.

This was an ambitious house and it was designed for Shuttleworth's clear vision about how he personally should live; he intended, for example, to change the colour of soft furnishings as the seasons changed. Unsurprisingly, it lingers in the mind like few others.

Timothy Brittain-Catlin

Elektra House

Architect: David Adjaye of Adjaye Associates
Location: Ashfield Street, Stepney, London

Stand before the uncompromisingly un-house-like front elevation of this seminal Adjaye work and it's not hard to believe it was controversial. What is surprising is that architects and planners kicked up the fuss, not residents. Architects were angered by its 'menacing windowless appearance' and warned the three-bedroom house wasn't suitable for children. They also doubted whether it was really built for £80,000 – just £614/sq m. To stay within this ascetic budget meant using innovative materials such as the Rothko-esque resin-coated plywood façade which prompted an apoplectic planning department to order its demolition. Thankfully a letter from Richard Rogers predicting Elektra would one day be seen as 'an example of its age' provided mollification.

In sharp contrast with its street-side blankness, the back is almost entirely glazed. Yet the clever internal layout means this isn't a gift for exhibitionists or voyeurs but effectively draws light into the unexpectedly bright and airy house.

Elizabeth Hopkirk

2001

Straw Bale House

Architect: Sarah Wigglesworth Architects
Location: Stock Orchard Street, London

Most of the unusual materials and technologies used in the Straw Bale House were chosen not because they are novel or to impress award judges but because they are cheap and accessible; the novelty lies in thinking to use them in this context.

This wonderful rambling farmhouse of a building is set beside one of the country's busiest railway lines – where the East Coast line approaches King's Cross, yet inside there is a calm that belies its setting and the eccentricity of the form. Cement bags buffer the office from noise, while the walls incorporate straw bales and gabion cages of recycled concrete.

Designed by Sarah Wigglesworth with Jeremy Till as their family home and office, it interested Kevin McCloud who included it in the first series of *Grand Designs*, drawing public attention to the hitherto dry and academic subject of sustainability. It also challenged the polite manners of contemporary modernism.

Tony Chapman

2002

BedZED

Architect: Bill Dunster and ZEDfactory
Location: Hackbridge, Surrey

ZED stands for Zero (fossil) Energy Development, and was a manifesto project commissioned by Peabody and the campaigning organisation Bioregional. BedZED was a major step towards housing that not only performed better in itself, but which, according to independent calculations, could help a willing resident to shift from the average ecological footprint equivalent to three planets to the only sustainable option – a one planet lifestyle.

Dwellings including family terrace houses and flats face south, while the northern face of the Zeilenbau rows is used for offices and live-work units, offering on-site employment to avoid commuting. Dunster focused on refining the cross-sections to achieve maximum solar harvesting without over-heating, aided by updraught stacks marked by roof cowls, which contain heat-exchangers. Most of the available technologies of the time for avoiding environmentally harmful sources of heating and cooling were deployed, but the greatest gains were achieved by passive methods.

Alan Powers

2003

Black Rubber House

Architect: Simon Conder Associates
Location: Dungeness, Kent

Take a moody, bleak setting – Dungeness – loomed over by the nuclear menace of a power station; take a 1930s fishing hut, strip it back to its timber frame, extend and clad it in a breathable yet waterproof material used for wetsuits; park an Airstream caravan next door as a guest wing, and you have a piece of architecture, which together with Derek Jarman's garden, kick-started an outpouring of brilliantly eccentric design that has opened up the wild bottom right-hand corner of England to the world.

Simon Conder's house for a couple of weekending Londoners is as warm and sophisticated inside as it is forbidding yet intriguing outside. The ingenuity of well-detailed ply fixtures and fittings make for a piece that raises the ante from beach hut to architecture. As Marco Goldschmied, who awarded it the Stephen Lawrence Prize said, 'it is extraordinary and ordinary at the same time'.

Tony Chapman

2004

Woodlands Crescent

Architect: Ben Pentreath
Location: Poundbury, Dorset

In Marmiteville Poundbury, taste reigns, whether you like it or not – or so it might appear. Ben Pentreath offers a sound basis in practical domestic planning in the Woodlands Crescent houses, with living kitchens running front to back on the ground floor, a raised living room above away from the fray, and the rest economically fitted in. Building in pairs saves space with entry from the side, while low-level link blocks create security and extra space. If the result is reminiscent of Michael Searles's Paragon development in Blackheath, 1793–1807, it has arrived by its own logic. The two schemes have in common a desire to avoid the fragmented look of paired villas and to create an ensemble, especially satisfying when they front onto a curved road. Although twenty-first-century builders are unfamiliar with refined mouldings and curves, Pentreath tests them to their limit, but not beyond.

Alan Powers

Brick House

Architect: Caruso St John Architects
Location: Westbourne Grove, London

The genius of Caruso St John's Brick House, which was shortlisted for the 2006 RIBA Stirling Prize, lay in its simplicity. On a land-locked site, rising only one storey out of the ground so as not to steal the neighbours' light, it reminded us of the gorgeousness of brick, a material previously long ignored by architects (what did they start? Now every office block, gallery and housing estate is made of the stuff.)

The eponymous bricks look as if they have done a turn or two already but in fact they are new. But the concrete is just as important inside and is left exposed to reveal the fractal geometries which in turn define the various uses of cooking, dining and sitting. These are architects who look at each building type afresh and here they have given something new and special to the typology of the one-off house.

Tony Chapman

The Framehouse

Architect: Marcus Lee
Location: Rowe Lane, Hackney, London

In 2000 Lee bought this wasteland plot behind Georgian terraces, and designed a flat-pack three-storey house framed in Siberian Larch for his family. The five-bedroom eco-home, with features such as an air-source heat pump and rainwater harvesting, was built in just six months, from digging drainage and laying foundations to moving in. The house won an RIBA award and featured on *Grand Designs*.

It has a wedge-shaped profile, opening out from a modest entrance to a huge open-plan reception room and kitchen at the back, with floor-to-ceiling glazing overlooking the garden. The layout was inspired by Japanese design, using every inch of space and concealing mundane necessities like the washing machine and a slim shower room in storage along the side walls. A wooden staircase rises through the centre of the house with rooms off it, avoiding corridors. None of the internal walls are load-bearing and the layout has already been modified to suit the family's needs.

Susannah Charlton

Gap House

Architect: Luke Tozer of Pitman Tozer Architects
Location: Monmouth Road, Paddington

Luke and Charlotte Tozer were expecting their first
child when they went house hunting, and found
a derelict 1950s cottage in a gap 8ft (2.4m) wide.
Their second son arrived four weeks after the
completion of its replacement 22 months later. Three
storeys of bedrooms, their windows proportioned
like those of the Victorian neighbours, are stacked
over the semi-basement entrance where a long
corridor opens into an L-shaped living and kitchen
space dug down where the plot broadens at the rear.
Above this double-height, top-lit space the house
steps back in a cascade of glass. More glazing folds
back onto a courtyard, paved with the limestone that
continues through the house, interrupted only by
a grille that collects rainwater to flush lavatories on
each floor, and access to boreholes feeding the heat
pump that provides heating and hot water. The deep
plan provides so much storage that even two growing
boys seem tidy.

Elain Harwood

Craddock Cottages

Architect: Stephen Taylor Architects
Location: Gomshall, Surrey

Some of the most influential British architects from the Gothic Revival onwards have urged their contemporaries to learn at first hand from vernacular building traditions. Stephen Taylor Architects have taken this advice more seriously than most, their work displaying not only close observation of the materials and construction methods of local buildings, but also of their organic evolution and form. These two houses on the busy road that connects Guildford with Dorking grew from a careful study of local cottages and the spaces between them, but at the same time have striking forms and details of their own, for example the decorative concrete lintels with their brick-fragment aggregate.

The houses won a RIBA award in 2009, and Stephen Taylor became *Building Design*'s Housing Architect of the Year. His recent group of houses in Crouch End demonstrates how well the same approach can suit a suburban setting.

Timothy Brittain-Catlin

2009

Tibby's Triangle

Architect: Ash Sakula
Location: Southwold, Suffolk

On part of the old Adnams Brewery site in Southwold, a flint's throw from the church of St Edmund, Ash Sakula designed a tightly gathered group of 34 homes, of which ten 'affordable' ones are scattered through the site. Facing the sea is a terrace with big windows boxed out at the top of the tall narrow houses for the view. Other buildings are more varied in height, some freestanding, some linked. A wide green lies at their feet, and most rise sheer from the ground. A 'shared space' roadway threads through the middle, widening to make space for an outdoor market, and the project includes a shop and café.

Vernacular but not twee, Tibby's Triangle exemplifies the best thinking of its time: sensitive, flexible, practical and visually stimulating. The architects Cany Ash and Robert Sakula and their studio are well known for their social engagement and their sense of fun.

Alan Powers

2010

The Meat Factory

Architect: Julian Marsh of Marsh Grochowski
Location: Felton Road, The Meadows, Nottingham

Marsh had collaborated on low-energy housing
with Nottingham University before, in 2005, he
and his partner, artist Jude Liebert, decided to
slowly rebuild a factory near the city centre as their
home. The V-shaped plan wedged between older
terraces opens its arms south-westwards, embracing
a courtyard and drawing warmth into a double-
height conservatory; partly glazed and partly clad in
recyclable polycarbonate, it is shaded by planting in
summer and insulated by Ecover bottles filled with
salt water. Behind is a studio, half double-height
for Liebert to exhibit her work, and a garage for an
electric car. Living accommodation is on the first
floor, with a balcony giving views over recreation
grounds towards the river. The Meat Factory is
highly insulated, yet can be opened up in summer,
while the energy use from photovoltaic cells beats
Passivhaus requirements. But unlike most eco-homes
featuring such technology, it is also beautiful.

Elain Harwood

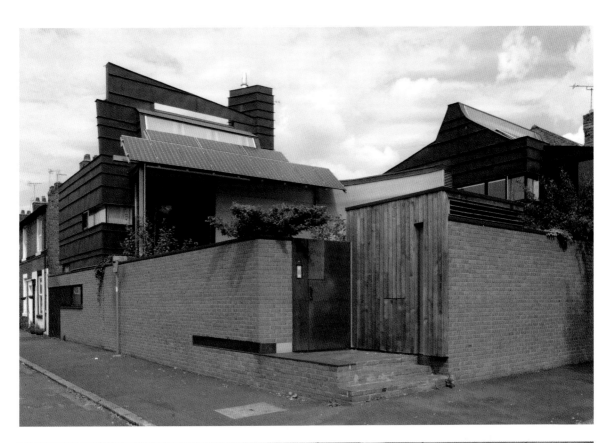

The Triangle

Architect: Glenn Howells Architects
Location: Northern Road, Swindon

Kevin McCloud is best known for his TV studies of the one-off house, but in Swindon he put his money where his mouth had been to create with Glenn Howells some exemplary housing that recalls the town's much-loved Victorian railway workers' cottages.

These cheap-as-chips houses don't look it because the meagre £4,200,000 million budget for the first phase of 42 houses (yes a build cost of £100,000 each) has been wisely spent on the detailing, the intelligent services and on a generous public realm. The architect worked hard to give the client value for money by achieving higher densities than originally planned.

The materials are rustic but in no way twee: galvanised steel porticos, gabion walls, unpainted rainwater pipes and prominent ventilation stacks that mimic chimneys. The house plans are compact but the clever section and the dropped sills mean they don't feel cramped. More social housing should be like this.

Tony Chapman

2012

South Chase, Newhall

Architect: Alison Brooks Architects
Location: Harlow, Essex

Frederick Gibberd planned Harlow as a series of
neighbourhoods based on the catchment of a junior
school. One new neighbourhood captures something
of the town's initial magic, developed by local
landowners Jon and William Moen to a master plan
by Roger Evans (Studio Real) that combines the
courtyard planning of the Essex Design Guide with
a bold palette of approved materials and finishes.
Some 3,000 dwellings are planned and one quadrant
is almost finished. Bids were invited from architect-
developer teams to raise the quality bar for volume
house building. The best group is the patio houses
on the southern edge, designed in 2007 by Brooks
working with Galliford Try to a tight plan of 52
units per 2.5 acres/1ha. Designed to a lower budget
than her award-winning Arcadia in Cambridge
of timber over ground-floor blockwork, they are
distinctive for their oblique pitched roofs and black
weatherboarding inspired by that of Essex barns.

Elain Harwood

House No.7

Architect: Denizen Works
Location: Isle of Tiree, Scotland

Building in the countryside presents problems enough; building on a remote Scottish island multiplies them. But Tiree has form for award-winning architecture. A ferry shelter-cum-art installation was shortlisted for the RIBA Stirling Prize in 2003. Then, in 2014, Murray Kerr of Denizen Works rebuilt one of the tumbledown black Hebridean houses for his parents and won the Stephen Lawrence Prize.

The three volumes of the house are linked by a glazed-roofed atrium, but they are separately expressed: the original house a black pitch-roofed white-rendered stone building, the two new elements have corrugated agricultural cladding that look the part. Yet inside all is cosy warmth provided by an air-source heat pump. Collectively they are corralled like farm animals hunched together against the weather.

Marco Goldschmied described it as 'an intelligent and witty response to the function and logistical challenges of location, orientation and isolation.' He was right.

Tony Chapman

2014

Covert House

Architect: Deborah Saunt and David Hills (DSDHA)
Location: Clapham, London

Covert House poses an interesting question given
London's housing crisis: could this diaphanous
mirror box be a model for acceptable densification?
Given the will, half the back gardens in suburbia
could have such a house, increasing the number
of homes without environmental destruction. To
win approval from planners and neighbours in a
conservation area Saunt concealed her home's scale
by burying one of its two storeys underground
and staggering the profile of its upper pavilion
so it swoops as low as the garden walls around it.
The partial loss of the garden plot is offset by new
planting and sustainable design. But the cleverest
mitigation is what makes it so entrancing. Glass
and mirrors work together like the camouflage
on a dazzle ship to confuse the eye and blur the
line between the built and the planted so even in
plain sight the house appears to dissolve into the
surrounding trees.

Elizabeth Hopkirk

2015

A House for Essex

Architect: Charles Holland, formerly of FAT
Location: Wrabness, Essex

A House for Essex is an amalgam of Grayson Perry's imagination and Charles Holland's ability to interpret those ideas into architectural form for Alain de Botton's Living Architecture project. It is, therefore, a house designed for short stays, and a house which tells the story of Perry's fictional Julie May Cope and her trajectory from Canvey Island to the University of Essex. The result is a small ceramic-clad, telescoping metal-roofed jewel box sited above the estuary of the River Stour as it meets the North Sea. Surprisingly, given the exuberant, almost overwrought, detailing of the exterior, the interior is flooded with natural light, the succession of dormer windows opening up the views, inland to a rolling arable landscape, or out towards the coast where a forest of cranes marks the massive port at Felixstowe. Without this cleverly chosen site, the creators' ambitions might have foundered but here it turns out to be, perfectly, at home.

Gillian Darley

Acknowledgements

C20 Society would like to thank all those who have contributed entries or photographs to this book. Particular thanks are due to Jennie Walmsley for her tireless work as the volunteer picture researcher.

Gerald Adler Professor and Deputy Head of Kent School of Architecture, University of Kent

John Allan Consultant architect to Avanti Architects, visiting professor of Sheffield University and Chairman of Isokon Gallery Trust

Lucy Archer Writer, lecturer and author of a monograph on her father, *Raymond Erith, Architect*

Timothy Brittain-Catlin Architect, historian, reader at the University of Kent and vice-chairman of the C20 Society

Barnabas Calder Teaches at University of Liverpool and writes on British Brutalism and Denys Lasdun

Louise Campbell Historian of art and architecture, Emeritus Professor, University of Warwick

Rutter Carroll Architect, academic and author of *Ryder and Yates* for the C20 Architects series

Tony Chapman Writer, film-maker and honorary fellow of the RIBA

Susannah Charlton Consultant and manager of the Twentieth Century Society's website

Catherine Croft Director of the Twentieth Century Society

Andrew Crompton Architectural historian and Reader at Liverpool School of Architecture

Gillian Darley Historian, journalist and president of the Twentieth Century Society

Harriet Edgerley Architect

Jonathan Ellis-Miller Architect

Alistair Fair Lecturer in Architectural History at the University of Edinburgh

Kathryn Ferry Independent architectural historian, writer and lecturer

Geraint Franklin Architectural historian with Historic England

Emily Gee London Planning Director at Historic England

Don Gray Professor and Head of the Kent School of Architecture

Edward Hagger A life member of the C20 Society who has researched the life and work of F. C. Eden

Elain Harwood Historian with English Heritage, author, and co-editor of the Twentieth Century Society Journal

Rosemary Hill Writer, historian and independent scholar

Wendy Hitchmough Head of Historic Buildings & Research, Historic Royal Palaces

Philip Hodgkinson Architect

Elizabeth Hopkirk Assistant Editor of Building Design

Lesley Jackson Writer and curator specialising in twentieth century design

Neil Jackson Architect, architectural historian and Charles Reilly Professor of Architecture at the University of Liverpool

Pat Kirkham Professor at Kingston University, and formerly Bard Graduate Center and De Montfort University, specialising in history of design, architecture and cultural studies. Owner of Goddard House since 2013.

Jill Lever Architectural historian

Fiona MacCarthy Biographer and historian, and former president of the Twentieth Century Society

Christine Hui Lan Manley Architectural practitioner, historian and author of *Frederick Gibberd* for the C20 Architects series

Debbie Mays Head of Listing at Historic England

Mervyn Miller Architect, town planner and leading expert on the early Garden City movement

Peter Murray Editor, author, curator and Chairman of New London Architecture and The London Society

Kenneth Powell Architectural critic, consultant and historian

Tess Pinto Conservation adviser for the C20 Society

Alan Powers Trustee and former chairman of the Twentieth Century Society, specialist in twentieth century British art and design

Clare Price Senior Conservation Adviser for the Twentieth Century Society

Sally Rendel Architect and co-author of *Connell, Ward and Lucas: Modern Movement Architects in England 1929-1939*

Elizabeth Robinson Author of *Lost Hackney* and *Twentieth century buildings in Hackney*. Editor of the *Victorian* (2004–13)

Lou Robson Prefab aficionado, writer, researcher and heritage consultant

Joanna Smith Historian with Historic England

Gavin Stamp Freelance architectural historian and former chairman of the C20 Society

Tony Stokoe Chair of the C20 South West Region

Neil Swanson Landscape Architect and owner of Cedarwood

Adam Voelcker Architect and author

Lynne Walker Architectural historian and Senior Research Fellow at the Institute of Historical Research, University of London; writes widely on gender, space and architecture.

Dennis Wardleworth Independent scholar

Matthew Wickens Architect and senior teaching fellow at the University of Bath

Further reading

John Allan, *Berthold Lubetkin, Architecture and the tradition of progress,* London, Black Dog, 2014

Lucy Archer, *Raymond Erith, Architect,* London, Cygnet Press, 1985

Timothy Brittain-Catlin, *Leonard Manasseh and Partners,* London, RIBA, 2010

Timothy Brittain-Catlin, *Bleak Houses: Disappointment and failure in Architecture,* Cambridge, MIT Press, 2014

Barnabas Calder, *Raw Concrete: The beauty of Brutalism*, London, Heinemann, 2016

Rutter Carroll, *Ryder and Yates*, London, RIBA, 2009

Tony Chapman, *The Stirling Prize: Ten years of architecture and innovation*, London, Merrell, 2006

Susannah Charlton & Elain Harwood, eds., *100 Buildings 100 Years*, London, Batsford, 2014

Gillian Darley & David McKie, *Ian Nairn: Words in Place*, Nottingham, Five Leaves, 2013

Kathryn Ferry, *The 1950s Kitchen*, London, Shire, 2011

Geraint Franklin, *Howell Killick Partridge and Amis*, London, Historic England, 2017

John Grindrod, *Concretopia*, London, Old Street Publishing, 2013

Elain Harwood, *Space, Hope and Brutalism: English Architecture 1945-75*, London, Yale University Press, 2015

Elain Harwood, *Chamberlin, Powell & Bon*, London, Historic England 2016

Elain Harwood & James O Davies, *England's Post-War Listed Buildings*, London, Batsford, 2015

Elain Harwood & Alan Powers, *Tayler and Green*, London, Prince of Wales Institute of Architecture, 1998

Elain Harwood & Alan Powers, eds., Twentieth Century Architecture 9: *Housing the Twentieth Century*, London, C20 Society, 2008

Elain Harwood & Alan Powers, Twentieth Century Architecture 12: *Houses: Regional Practice and Local Character*, London, C20 Society, 2015

Wendy Hitchmough, *The Arts and Crafts Home*, London, Pavilion, 2000

Wendy Hitchmough, *C F A Voysey*, London, Phaidon, 1997

Lesley Jackson, *Modern British Furniture: Design since 1945*, London, V & A, 2013

Lesley Jackson, *Contemporary: Architecture and interiors of the 1950s*, London, Phaidon, 1994

Lesley Jackson, *The Sixties*, London, Phaidon, 1998

Neil Jackson, *The Modern Steel House,* London, E. & F. N. Spon, 1996

Christine Manley, *Frederick Gibberd*, London, Historic England, 2017

Fiona MacCarthy, *British Design since 1880: A visual history*, London, Lund Humphries, 1982

Mervyn Miller, *English Garden Cities: An introduction,* London, English Heritage, 2010

Kenneth Powell, *Powell & Moya,* London, RIBA, 2009

Kenneth Powell, *Ahrends Burton and Koralek*, London RIBA, 2012

Alan Powers, *The Twentieth Century House in Britain, from the archives of* Country Life, London, Aurum Press, 2004

Alan Powers, *Modern: The Modern Movement in Britain*, London, Merrell, 2005

Alan Powers, *Britain: Modern architectures in history*, London, Reaktion, 2007

Alan Powers, *Aldington, Craig & Collinge*, London, RIBA, 2009

Elizabeth Robinson, *Twentieth Century Buildings in Hackney*, London, Hackney Society, 1999

Dennis Sharp & Sally Rendel, *Connell, Ward and Lucas: A Modernist Architecture in England*, London, Frances Lincoln, 2008

Gavin Stamp, *Edwin Lutyens Country Houses, from the archives of Country Life*, London, Aurum, 2012

Gavin Stamp, 'Neo-Tudor and its enemies', in *Architectural History*, vol.49, 2006

Gavin Stamp, *Twentieth Century Architecture 2: The Modern House Revisited*, London, C20 Society, 1996

Adam Voelcker, *Herbert Luck North: Arts and Crafts Architecture for Wales*, RCAHM, Wales, 2011

Index